PRA
THE LAST PARENTING
BOOK YOU'LL EVER READ

"As parents, how do we evolve from the 'arms full' to the 'hands free' stage of family life, as our children leave the nest? With cutting-edge research, practical suggestions, humor, and many stories from her own experience as the mother of a big family, writer Meagan Francis provides an invaluable resource for anyone making this bittersweet transition—with both its pitfalls and its possibilities."

—Gretchen Rubin, bestselling author of *The Happiness Project* and host of the *Happier with Gretchen Rubin* podcast

"For anyone who went into parenting with the vague idea that the aim was to successfully get the kids to their 18th birthdays (or college graduation) in one piece and then—ta-da!—you'd be at the finish line, this book feels like a wise, compassionate, and necessary reality check. In sharing her own experience parenting teens and launching young adults, Francis gives a full picture of this bumpy and beautiful phase of motherhood—and midlife—while inviting us to reclaim parts of ourselves that took a backseat during the more intensive early years. I *loved* this book, and the reminder that my role as mom is shifting, not ending; that it's important *and* imperfect; and that I can take small steps now to create a rich, fulfilling life when, someday, the nest is truly empty."

—Sarah Powers, co-host of *The Mom Hour* podcast

"Meagan Francis has long been one of my go-tos for smart parenting advice. Hers is the voice I want in my ear as my family—and I—move into this new phase, and I promise you will too."

—KJ Dell'Antonia, *New York Times* bestselling author

"Is there anything better than hearing from an honest and relatable mom who has been there, done that? Packed with hard-won wisdom, charming anecdotes, and reflective insights, The Last Parenting Book You'll Ever Read offers much-needed light at the end of the parenting-young-kids tunnel. Thank you, Meagan, for taking us under your wing."

—Ashlee Gadd, founder of Coffee + Crumbs and author of *Create Anyway: The Joy of Pursuing Creativity in the Margins of Motherhood*

The LAST PARENTING BOOK

You'll Ever Read

The LAST PARENTING BOOK

You'll Ever Read

HOW WE LET OUR KIDS GO AND EMBRACE WHAT'S NEXT

Meagan Francis

Published by Sourcebooks
P.O. Box 4410, Naperville, Illinois 60567-4410
(630) 961-3900
sourcebooks.com

Cataloging-in-Publication Data is on file with the Library of Congress.

Printed and bound in the United States of America
VP 10 9 8 7 6 5 4 3 2 1

To my mother, who would be proud.

CONTENTS

Part 2: What's Ahead

INTRODUCTION

I didn't want to write this book.

As a mother of five kids, a longtime parenting writer, and cohost of *The Mom Hour* podcast, I've been creating content about motherhood for more than twenty years—and *living* motherhood for twenty-seven. After a long hiatus from authoring books, when I started thinking about writing another, I was tempted to make a clean exit from the parenting genre.

Four of my five kids are adults, and the youngest will graduate from high school in a few years. I thought that meant I was ready to mentally leap forward, shifting the focus away from my role of Mom while I start planning a life full of the international travel, retirement-style leisure, and sparkling-clean countertops a parent can experience for any length of time only once her kids have all left home.

These things all seem so near I can practically taste them.

After all, of my five offsprings' combined ten feet, six (feet, that is) are *literally* out the door already, with my son Owen's half in, half out in the way of college students who still have a bedroom at home. And even though I'll still have one kid—my daughter, Clara—at home for the next few years, there's something daunting (and more than a little deflating) about the idea of parenting a lone teenager who'd really rather be following in her brothers' footsteps *now*, thankyouverymuch.

But as I struggled to get traction on a book idea that was focused on the next stage of life after active motherhood, I finally realized: I can't write that book yet…because I'm not there yet.

As much as I might have liked the idea of skipping neatly over the messy—and often painful—reality of transitioning out of this stage of my life and into the next, that's not, it turns out, how it actually works.

It took me years to adjust to being a mother of small kids; to surrender to the reality of giving up my sleep and bodily space and freedom and autonomy in service of a greater mission, the deeper sense of joy and purpose that, for me, accompanied the house-full phase of motherhood. So it only makes sense that it would take years to adjust to releasing it all in order to move onto something else: a stage that's a lot freer and less physically demanding and much better rested, yes, but also the absence of a certain sweetness to which I became accustomed.

Some days it feels exhilarating; other days, demoralizing. And if you're reading this book, you're likely experiencing some of these same emotions.

Amid all the conflicting feelings in this moment, I'm working to find a middle ground that allows me to face the long goodbye without completely losing myself in it, a road that makes it possible to set myself up for a happy, healthy, and fulfilled life after parenting while still creating strong, lifelong bonds with my kids. This is the premise and promise of *The Last Parenting Book You'll Ever Read*.

It's my hope that sharing my experience will both help you feel less alone and also give you a framework for how to approach your own transition during this time of life, by distilling what I'm learning—and have learned—into a blend of gentle advice and simple recognition of where you are in this stage of motherhood. By identifying your own needs, and imagining a new kind of motherhood identity, you can develop a road map to reinventing your relationships with yourself, your kids, and the world around you.

Through *The Mom Hour* podcast, which I've cohosted for ten years with my friend and fellow big-kid mom Sarah Powers, and my other online writing and community, I hear from so many women in this stage who feel as though their lives are on the precipice of change. Sometimes their youngest baby just entered middle or high school, and they feel uncertain about their identity beyond being a mother of small kids. Sometimes they're facing a big birthday—and the realization that they're no longer the "young mom" in the school pickup line. Other times they're simply dealing with the hormonal shifts of perimenopause while trying to keep it all together for a growing family.

These mothers also sense that there's a shift on the horizon: a redefinition of their identities as mother, woman, friend, and partner. They wonder how to make the most of the time, energy, and focus that their children's burgeoning independence will open up while experiencing some combination of excitement and sadness over how much their future roles as mothers will start to change.

This period of parenting is an opportunity to develop a new kind of relationship with our children and with the role of motherhood in our lives. It's an opportunity to help our kids prepare for adulthood while simultaneously preparing ourselves for the life on the other side as we "come of age" as mothers, learning to harness some of the mothering energy we've been directing toward our children and redirect it back toward nurturing *ourselves.*

This book follows my journey—still ongoing but nearing the end—from being a mom of many kids under one roof to a mom in a much smaller household, and the ways I'm using what I'm learning to prepare for the so-called "empty nest."

Let's dive in together.

Changes, redefinitions, and reinventions

There was a solid decade of my life where nothing really seemed to change all that much. Sure, there were changes happening around me all the time: We moved several times; I switched up my career; I kept having babies, and those babies kept getting older.

But for years, the basic flavor of life seemed to stay the same: I was mostly at home, surrounded by small people; and our lives followed a mostly predictable pattern of school drop-offs and pickups, naps and diaper changes, chaotic family dinners and piles of dishes.

All that seemed to shift when my oldest kids started high school. As their focus turned increasingly outward, I struggled to find my groove in this new version of family life. And the changes seemed to speed up, increasingly impacting the rhythms and routines of my day-to-day life as well as my relationships with my kids and my spouse at the time. Then, when my oldest was a newly minted high-school graduate and my youngest was in second grade, their father and I divorced—a dramatic shift that seemed to abruptly reflect the changes I'd long felt bubbling under the surface.

Over the next seven or eight years, the changes came fast and furious. Every two or three years another child graduated from high school and flew (or crawled) from the nest—but the pandemic complicated things, throwing our routines for a loop and also thwarting a couple of my older kids' fledgling attempts to launch. Then, in spring of 2023, I married Eric, my second husband. We'd been dating for three years by then, and while we were both more than ready to make it official, moving Clara and Owen—the only two kids still living at home at that point—into Eric's home required a large adjustment for all of us.

Even if you aren't facing something as dramatic as a divorce or remarriage, my guess is that you've also experienced the feeling that your life is on the precipice of an unwelcome, perhaps unexpected change. You sense that a reinvention is needed: a redefinition of your identity as mother, woman, friend, and partner. You're wondering how to use the time, energy, and focus that your kids' shifting needs will open up while experiencing some combination of excitement and sadness over how much your future as a mother will start to change.

A disclaimer right up front: **this isn't a parenting manual**. As Sarah and I have said in the intro to *The Mom Hour* for the past ten years, "We aren't experts—we're moms who've been there." And even with all the "been there" in my background, I often struggle to know exactly what to do in the circumstances where our modern world throws us.

How could I not? None of us grew up in a world like the one we, and our kids, inhabit today. My mother, who died in 1999, could never have fathomed a world of smartphones and social media or the ensuing pressure and anxiety they can cause. She likely never considered opioid addiction as a particular concern on my high-school campus (to my knowledge, she didn't have much reason to). It would never have occurred to her that any of her children might question their gender identity, dream of being a famous social media influencer, compete with artificial intelligence for their first job, or face many of the other issues today's parents face.

Of course many of these same concerns were around in the '80s and '90s, but there's no doubt that the way these issues—as well as mental health, addiction, and others—are playing out among teens and young adults has changed rapidly and dramatically. No wonder none of us are exactly sure how to navigate it all. If you're looking for that professional guidance, there are experts in this space who can help you learn to be a more effective parent to adolescents and young adults: Lisa Damour, Kenneth Ginsburg, and Jessica Lahey are three who come to mind.

What I *can* offer insight on is the experience of being a mother, my primary identity and the focus of my work and my world for nearly three decades now. And while I will typically stop shy of telling you *how* to parent, I am here to walk alongside you on this particular part of the parenthood path: the part where you're reaching the end of something and wondering what's next.

At some point along the circuitous journey of parenting, we're charting a whole new course where our paths run alongside our child's, occasionally overlapping but not completely intertwined. And where those disparate paths will take us, together and separately, is anyone's guess and—here's the catch—not always something we can control.

Those paths might include developing friendships with our children, or providing them with welcomed mentorship…or, maybe, grappling with painful distance. At different points along the way, many of us will experience all three. This journey also asks us to examine our own lives and motives and to ask ourselves hard questions about our choices, our identities, and what we want and need and expect from life when our children are no longer at its center.

First-lasts, last-lasts, and what comes next

Okay, so this probably isn't *literally* the last parenting-related book you'll ever read. Maybe you've got a few more in you (especially if one day you're a grandparent struggling to remember what those early days in the trenches were like). But one thing is certain: at some point, *some* parenting book you read will be the last, just like all the other "lasts" you have experienced and will experience.

Some of these milestones are well marked and give us plenty of warning, like your youngest child's last first day of school. But so many of them are unmarked and unrecognized, until we look back and realize how long it's been since we were able to swing a child up on a hip or into the shopping cart, the last time they wanted to go trick-or-treating, the last time they fit into a child's-size shoe (and oh, how the bank account groans when they start shopping in the adult section!).

The beautiful thing about *lasts* is that they make room for so many lovely, life-changing, surprising *firsts*. Those include big milestones, like the first vacation you and your spouse go on where you don't have to worry about lining up childcare or rides to school and practice and work, as well as the subtler changes, like the first time you make it through a whole weekend without feeling the urge to check in on your college-age kid.

Lasts can be sad, scary, and confusing. They can be freeing, exciting, and wonderful. Often they are both. And in the years leading up to our children leaving home, they are constant.

Even after your offspring have moved on to life beyond your home, there will continue to be lasts: the last time your child sleeps in their childhood bed, maybe, or the last time everyone comes home for Christmas at the same time, or the last time your family goes on a trip together, just you and your kids, without partners or children of their own. Right now I find myself on a constant watch for these kinds of lasts, never sure which holiday or gathering might be the last of its sort.

As a mother of five, I have experienced countless lasts, and those lasts seem to compound in significance with the youngest child. Sure, with each of Clara's older brothers, there was a last time I nursed them or changed their diapers or dropped them off at kindergarten. But Clara was my *last* last. And while the faint question of "Well, what if there's another baby one day…?" accompanied many of the babyhood lasts, I had a hysterectomy when Clara was four years old—after which I became hyperaware of the significance of each of the lasts.

With her, my youngest, there were so many obvious ones: my last day with a child aged in the single digits, my last day with a child in elementary school (this milestone was all but wrecked by the pandemic), my last day with a preteen. And unlike when I went through these lasts with her older brothers, as they happen with

Clara I'm very aware that there's no next-younger sibling to bring up the rear and ease the sting.

For years, when the boys were going through sullen or withdrawn stages in adolescence or just off doing their own thing, I could count on sweet little Clara to be my ringer: always eager for a snuggle on the sofa, always happy to accompany me wherever I went. Those days slipped behind me without so much as a whisper of warning, and I've reproached myself often for squandering them. When was the last time Clara tried to climb into my bed late at night? Did I rebuff her or invite her with a warm embrace? (I hope I invited her in, but let's face it—her elbows used to become lethal weapons at 2 a.m.)

Not long ago I asked Clara if she'd like to snuggle up in my bed with me and watch a movie, and for a moment I saw her face contort into the same pity-filled look you'd give a matted, toothless stray cat that wants to come home with you. After a moment of struggle, she got her features under control and simply said, "Ehhh, not really"—kindly, yet leaving zero room to be convinced. It was like having your party invitation rejected by the nicest popular girl in junior high—sure, she didn't go out of her way to be mean about it, but afterward you felt like a fool for asking.

My oldest son left home for the first time eight years ago (he's come back several times; more on that later), and since then, one by one, his younger siblings have grown and flown. So I have plenty of practice with the long goodbye. But *this*, as the kids say, hits different. All my kids eventually finished elementary school, grew out of their snuggle-with-Mom stage, or became teenagers; but as long as I still had *one*, I was still in the game. And now, as I face down the mother of all lasts—my last child's last few years under my roof—I realize that for me, these years will truly be the last gasps of mothering, an experience and identity I will have carried day in and day out for *thirty years* by the time Clara starts her adult life.

Last year, we passed another last—Clara started high school. Shortly thereafter, her brother Owen headed off to college, and Clara and I began counting down the days until a triple-whammy last— the last day before my last child turns eighteen, followed quickly by that same last child's very last day of high school, followed quickly by wherever life takes her after that.

Still my daughter, of course. Still *my* child, but no longer *a* child. And…then what?

As I embarked on this final but oh-so-important stage of parenting, I identified areas of my life that would need attention in order for me to make the transition, as well as some key actions I'd need to take to shore up my foundation. I'd need to nurture a strong sense of my identity as a woman and person outside of motherhood. I'd need to reexamine assumptions I may have made about how parent-teen relationships "should" look and what my children "owe" me (and I them). I'd need to address my own health goals, and career, and lifestyle, and relationships and decide what was next for *me*.

And I learned that the biggest challenge during this transition might be to stay present and fully invested without trying to freeze time—or trying to freeze out my nurturing side. It meant keeping my eyes open to opportunities to bond with my kids and my heart open to the pain and disappointment of possible (let's be honest, *probable*) rejection. It would mean seeking adventure and learning and growth instead of shrinking into myself. And it would mean letting go—*so, so* much letting go.

I know I'm not in the clear yet. There's plenty more upheaval to grapple with ahead as my older kids go through the inevitable trials and challenges of adulthood and I help my youngest two launch into the world—not to mention my own menopause journey, which is still a question mark at this point. But being a bit on the precocious side when it comes to going through the stages of motherhood (in other words, I started young and crammed in a lot of baby making in a relatively short period of time) means I have the benefit of being a bit earlier to this stage than most other women my age.

This stage of motherhood—kids one foot out the door but not fully flown yet—presents us with so many opportunities to seek growth, self-awareness, personal fulfillment, creative challenges, and more. But to do this, we need to be willing to shake things up. We may have to redefine our mothering identities and roles so we don't get stuck in the old "muscle memory" of motherhood, continuing to play out our old roles because we don't know how to move forward. We may need to rethink the parenting strategies that worked so well when the children were littler, or examine beliefs about how we think young adults "should" be parented in the face of lived experience as evidence to the contrary.

As someone who's spent a career telling young mothers to trust their instincts because "it's all gonna be okay"—another oft-repeated motto at *The Mom Hour* podcast—I hope that at the very least, when you get to the end of this book, you'll feel reassured that all this work you've put in as a mother has been for a purpose and that this often confusing stage, which can be so full of disillusionment, has a purpose, too.

Either way, I hope that within these pages you'll find

encouragement to take a deep breath and let your children grow into the people they are meant to be…so that you can do the same for yourself.

Part 1

LOOKING BACK

C an I tell you something that I hope you'll find reassuring? This—whatever *this* means for you right now—won't last forever.

No matter which stage you're in right now, that statement is true. If you're reading this book, you've likely moved past the point where you're nursing an infant while a two-year-old choke-holds you from behind while trying to scale your back. And you've also probably moved past the blessed stage in which your kids were sleeping normal hours at night and readily expressing their love for you with verbal praise and physical affection.

Chances are good the stage you're in now is different from those earlier days in some pretty key ways. Maybe your kid still sleeps long hours but during an inconvenient window that starts about three hours after you've gone to bed and, if left to their own devices, would extend about five hours past the beginning of the school day. All kinds of weird smells emanate from their bedroom and laundry pile. Those things might be manageable if not for the fact that you're pretty sure your kid despises you right now: hiding in that weird-smelling bedroom or behind a screen, speaking primarily in grunts, or not at all.

It will pass; I promise you, it will.

You may also be experiencing a stage of parenting marked by despair. A stage that perhaps requires the help of experts to help you and your child sort it out...and even then, there may be no guarantees of ease for your child or resolution of the tension in your relationship. Would you believe me, while you're so thick in the confusion of grappling with your child's struggles and perhaps hostility, if I told you that this stage will also eventually be a thing of the past?

It's also true. Whatever struggles lie in the future, this—this particular manifestation, this singular moment you're in—this, too, shall pass.

There's another stage, as well, one that's potentially the most disorienting of all. It's the stage when *your* child is no longer, in fact, *a* child. They live somewhere besides your home and spend their days with people you don't know, in places you've never been. Their comings and goings and sayings and doings are mostly a mystery. Even if you have a strong relationship with said not-a-child child, even if you keep in regular touch, the majority of this emerging adult person's day-to-day life will be unknown to you and unseen by you. Unless they have a uniquely dependent relationship with you, your nonchild child will be beyond your direct influence in matters such as choosing the correct outerwear for the day's weather forecast, turning handles inward when heating a pot of water on the stovetop, or considering which potential mate they might want to consider swiping right.

Believe it or not, this stage will also pass. Not because your once-flown fledgling will be moving back in with you (though that's certainly possible and may even be desirable, as we'll cover in "The Truth About the Empty Nest") or because they'll willingly subject themselves to your opinions on every one of their life decisions (less likely and vastly less desirable; see "Big Kids, Big Problems, Big Fat Worry"), but because, whatever version of your and your adult child's relationship is right now, it will change—and it will continue to change for as long as you both are alive.

In the first half of this book, we'll spend some time exploring our quickly changing roles as parents. We'll explore topics such as parental pride, what we remember (and what we don't), our own motherhood regrets, and the ways our parenting philosophy and roles must change—whether we like it or not—as our kids get older and more independent.

No matter where you are in your parenting journey right now, two things are certain: you can't ever go back to any of the stages that came before, and where you're going is often a mystery. I think of the transition from early, active motherhood to the next stage as going "from arms full to hands free," and it's what opens up the space to explore what's next in our lives both as mothers and more-than-mothers. Let's start there.

FROM ARMS FULL TO HANDS FREE

There was a time, not so long ago, when I was completely drowning in small children. Five, to be exact; four boys and then a girl, a wild tangle of limbs intertwined on the sofa and a mad tumble down the stairs on Christmas mornings. There was nearly always a pair of little arms clinging to my legs or a possessive hand stuck down the front of my shirt (if you've breastfed, you probably know what I'm talking about).

In those days I read books and blogs written by mothers whose children had grown and flown and knew, logically, that would also be my future—but I couldn't quite believe it in my bones. I felt that stage of life—what I now call the "arms-full" stage—right down to the core of my being.

At that time, children were *omnipresent* for me: they filled my physical, mental, and emotional space. Their toys filled the living room, the kitchen cabinets were a messy jumble of their brightly colored utensils, and their small clothes routinely made their way into my drawers. My to-do lists were defined by child-related tasks, my published writing mostly explored the experience of motherhood, and my social media posts were full of funny or charming things my kids had done. My car, my bed, my hard drive, my arms…typically, all were full of children.

And mothering, in the arms-full stage, is *intimate*. Small children make themselves known. Through verbal protest or bodily demonstration, they share with us how they feel about pretty much everything: the seams in their socks; our skills at playing make-believe (which don't meet their expectations, if your kids are anything like mine were); the dinner we lovingly crafted, only for it to grow cold, dry, and mostly untouched on the table. We're acutely aware of their bodies, too: how clean or dirty they are, or how fast they're growing, yes, but also how small changes can indicate a disruption in the system, like a rash after their bath or a slight change in the quality of a cough.

And as a result of all the mental gymnastics that go along with the above, a mother's mind becomes a well-oiled and carefully sharpened tool, adept at both anticipating and heading off problems before they arise as well as tuning out noise, chaos, and odors. When my arms were full of little ones, I'd become a master at the anticipatory duck-and-swerve: moving swiftly to prevent a chubby baby arm from knocking over a full cup of milk or taking evasive action to keep a toddler's sniffles from escalating into a full-on Target tantrum.

My experience of motherhood has changed dramatically since the arms-full day when I forgot I'd ever had a life prior to it: a life before trash cans full of bagged-up diapers and drawers jammed by sippy cup lids, shirts decorated with milk stains and feet impaled by tiny plastic building blocks.

So while I'm still the mother of five humans now, one of whom still live under my roof and depend on me for their food, transportation, and internet connection, my daily experience of motherhood now would be almost unrecognizable to the arms-full me of fifteen years ago. My heart is still full—my children are smart, funny, kind people who I'm proud to have parented, who I love to be around—and they also worry and anger and disappoint and frustrate me on the regular.

There is no shortage of emotion in my current parenting life. My brain is still full too, with the logistical details that are part of my current stage of parenting: driver's ed schedules and high-school transcripts and FAFSA application deadlines and the late-start schedule that our school district inexplicably follows on *most* Wednesdays but not *all* Wednesdays.

But my arms? They're mostly empty, except for when I can convince one of my offspring to come in for a hug.

It's a bittersweet shift. I love the quiet, orderly, spacious life I inhabit now. But I also miss—intensely, sometimes—the sweetness of nursing a soft-cheeked baby, the sloppy kisses and squeezy hugs of an adoring toddler, the slow, gentle excitement of discovering nature during a neighborhood walk with a not-yet-jaded preschooler. I miss the easy readiness with which my elementary-age children would still come in for a hug or hang out on my bed while we each read, and even the midnight visits from a nearly-adolescent who, somehow prescient of the coming change, would seek refuge from the world with a cuddle in my bed. None of those things are a regular part of my life anymore, and I feel their absence deeply, in the same primal place in my heart that aches when I hear a toddler giggle at a restaurant or walk past the baby section at the store.

But it's not just the tinier versions of my specific children that I miss: it's the whole season of life. There was a sacred singularity to the arms-full phase of motherhood, and while I sensed that specialness when I was in it, I couldn't fully appreciate its significance until later.

Unlike the chaotic and crowded days of my arms-full stage, the hours today stretch out in front of me in a way that can seem luxurious—or lonely, depending on my mood and perspective. On weekends, I am the one who wakes my kids up, not the other way around, and if I leave the house for a few hours, they barely even notice. The house is usually quiet, tidy, and serene in a way it simply couldn't be when it was overrun with primary-color toys and blanket forts.

Just as in those younger days, life as a mom of older kids still brings surprises, both good and bad. But when your kids are bigger, those surprising moments tend to be fewer in number but far more dramatic in scale. Like finding out that your high schooler made a thoughtless, stupid comment on social media and now faces the possibility of serious disciplinary action. Or that your fifth grader has been getting bullied all year and finally worked up the guts to tell you. Or that your twelve-year-old *is* the bully, and their victim just got up the courage to tell *their* parents, who are now informing you. Or that your adult child ran out of money a few months ago and has been living in their car. Or that your tenth grader is miserably depressed and having suicidal thoughts. Or that your middle schooler and their friends decided to roam around town late at night and got picked up by the police. (I won't elaborate much to protect the not-so-innocent, but at least half of the previous events have been part of my parenting experience…and that last one happened on *two separate occasions*, to two different kids.)

I wasn't ready for how much adolescence changed my relationship with my kids. I, once the cuddliest of mothers, for whom cosleeping, extended nursing, and plenty of hugs were staples of my parenting toolbox, now sometimes have to remind myself that my teenage children will not actually disintegrate if I touch them. Likewise, I was unprepared for the way my kids stopped reflexively communicating their likes and dislikes, needs and preferences. How they no longer automatically brought me their problems and concerns; how I had to start looking for ways to seek them out and create a nonjudgmental and welcoming space for them to share.

So these days, my mothering reflexes feel a lot less catlike than they once did. As my control over my kids' choices has gone down, it seems the stakes of those choices have gone up, up, up. I'm slower to anticipate, and get in front of, problems because I'm not sure which *new* problems might possibly arise. In the arms-full stage, my kids were around and with me all the time; we shared a single universe. But as their universes have slowly expanded beyond mine, I've started losing track of them: not only of the threads that make up the fabric of their worlds, but also of any immediate impact on their day-to-day lives.

My four older kids live outside of my home, all pursuing lives that are unaffected by the quality of my breakfast pancakes or my ability to remember their bedtime hug. Clara's life, as a high-school sophomore, is also mysterious to me. We share fleeting meals around the dinner table in the evening or a quick chat in the morning before school. Soon enough, she'll have flown as well, and I'll be the one adjusting to a life completely different from the one I've known for nearly three decades. With all these changes, it's become much harder to feel confident that I've "done my job" at the end of the day—or what my job even *is*.

But I've been here before—and so, most likely, have you. As a new mom, I felt alternately insecure, inadequate, trapped, lonely, and exhausted. But as I settled into parenthood and got my sea legs under me, those feelings were mostly replaced by a sense of purpose: I had been entrusted with the care and keeping of these small people, and as it turned out, *I was pretty good at it.* As I grew more and more competent and confident in those skills, I also became more inspired to create a safe, nurturing, and joyful world for my kids to inhabit. Motherhood sparked my imagination like a good piece of fiction, and I was the author of our own unique and magical family story.

It's easy to romanticize early parenthood. Discovering the world through our children's eyes, we, in a way, feel like children. We have the power to create a world for them, and there is a sense of magic and wonder in that realization.

And while my life started to feel a little bit physically easier as my kids entered the teen years, for a while it also felt decidedly less fun. But that was simply a failure of my imagination. I've realized I can't let the magic disappear from my life just because my kids aren't as easily wowed or don't seem as enthusiastic about every idea I suggest. It is possible, I believe, to recover the sense of wonder and joy that may have gotten a little trampled by the hurt feelings we swallow down when our hug is deflected or our "Hi there!" is met with a grunt. We have the opportunity to create magic for *ourselves* now.

And though it's natural for our confidence to take a hit when we can no longer solve every one of our children's problems with a cuddle and an ice-cream cone, with practice and time we can once again regain a sense of purpose, confidence, and skill. *We can get good at this part!*

And we can layer on something new, too: an investment in our own selves that may just not have been possible during the arms-full stage.

Managing this transition means restoring balance in areas that have gotten knocked out of equilibrium as we've been shifting from the arms-full stage to the hands-free stage. It means developing new reflexes, learning once again to trust our intuition, developing confidence in the skills we have sharpened, and applying them in new ways to our current parent-child relationships.

It means looking for new ways to experience intimacy with kids who aren't necessarily available for (or interested in) a cuddle on the sofa, and new opportunities to lean into the joy and wonder of witnessing our children experiencing the world and making it their own: similar to the way we did when they were babies, only on a different sort of scale and with very different responsibilities and expectations.

It also means practicing self-nurturing, redirecting some of that mothering energy we've spent decades expending on our kids back toward ourselves.

As a young mother, I learned an important lesson: while my kids' developmental stages do, of course, impact me, I also needed to create a foundation in myself that would allow me to transcend the harder parts. And while I'm still working my way through this stage of life and its ever-shifting sands—one child in, another one out; this one flourishing, that one struggling—I've learned to once again find my balance. In the following chapters, we'll explore together some ideas that may help you regain yours, too.

Remember: we mothers in this middle stage still have a magical story to tell…and we are still its authors. With our hands free, we now have the space to write the story we've always wanted to live.

YOUR NEW PARENTING JOB DESCRIPTION

―――――――

t feels impossible sometimes to reconcile the fact that I've been a mother for more than a quarter century. I'll admit: for the past several years I've been feeling a bit pigeonholed in my role as Mom. Not only has discussing motherhood been the main thrust of my career, but *living* motherhood has dominated almost my entire adult life. With my kids quickly gaining independence, I often find myself seesawing wildly between a desire to go back in time to when they were little and I was the benevolent sun to their orbiting planets and an urge to jump forward to the next version of what my life will look like.

The most disorienting part about all of this is that my very identity as a mother is changing.

It all begs the question: Will I still be a mother when my kids no longer want or need any mothering at all? What, after all, is motherhood without an object?

For much of my life raising kids, my job as a parent seemed both maddeningly endless and reassuringly finite. Everyday struggles, from tantrums in Target to blowout diapers to tugs-of-war over coveted toys, turned my days into a series of small, specific, action-filled moments. Monotonous, yes, but also fast-moving, without a whole lot of time to reflect on whether I'd handled each situation perfectly in the moment.

Parenting doesn't look much like that anymore. There are still lots of small moments in my family's life, sure, but they seem a lot less self-contained. The decisions my kids and I discuss these days, around topics like college and careers, money and marriage, are simultaneously higher-stakes and slower-moving. It could be years before I know whether today's dinner-table conversations have any impact at all. I may *never* know.

A single day no longer feels like an endless smorgasbord of miniature three-act plays starring my children and myself as protagonist and antagonist (which person in which role depending on who's telling the story) but a slow, meandering novel in which problems spill over from chapter to chapter with no resolution in sight. Sometimes it's just a multiple-page monologue. (Yes, as my mother often said when I was in high school, parenting teens—often does feel like I'm talking to myself.)

Maybe that's why, even though everything about my life is easier—on paper at least—than it was when I had five young children to shepherd through a day, nothing about it seems simple anymore. And that's partly because what I'm doing often looks a lot less like what I'd define as "parenting" and more like something else entirely: something without clearly defined roles and expectations, without a well-marked path to follow.

What do you call a relationship where you aren't responsible for feeding or clothing a person, can offer advice or guidance only when it is requested, and have no real metric by which to judge your success? Here are some ways you might find your identity shifting as your kids get older.

From overseer to facilitator

Back in my arms-full days, buying and organizing school supplies was an hours-long process. First, I'd compile as many as five kids' supply lists into a single document, which I'd take to the store along with a child helper to check items off the list as I tossed them into the cart (one, and only one, helper was ideal; any more than that and the whole process tended to become a chaotic free-for-all).

At home, I'd put five brown paper sacks on the dining-room table—each labeled with a child's name—and then I'd chuck crayons and colored pencils and No. 2 pencils and mechanical pencils and pencil sharpeners and pencil cases and rubber erasers and fancy craft erasers and safety scissors and glue and paste and mucilage and rubber cement and watercolor paints and poster paints and tissues and hand sanitizer and rulers and protractors and notebooks and composition books and loose paper and three-ring folders and pocket folders and pocket three-ring folders into the appropriate bag, again cross-checking the list as I went. It was a hassle, but an enjoyable hassle, the sort of little nurturing ritual with a specific beginning and concrete ending that I came to love as a mother.

This school year, by comparison?

Clara snagged a three-subject notebook and pack of pens at the supermarket (after I cajoled her into going with me) and then referred to that paltry haul as her "supplies." Not a brightly colored logo or pencil case in sight.

The back-to-school period used to be an exciting if somewhat chaotic circus marked by ice-cream socials and fundraiser forms, extensive supply lists and the always-expensive act of replenishing the snack basket. But for the past several years—since my youngest child finished elementary school, really—the work required of me at the start of the school year has dwindled away. Now it's nearly nothing. A single high-school sophomore just doesn't create much chaos at the beginning of a new year. She chooses her own clothes, buys her own supplies, manages her own calendar. At most, I might be asked to supply a ride.

Is it a welcome change? It certainly seems like it *should* be. Getting five kids ready to start the school year in three different schools was a logistical challenge that taxed both my physical energy and organizational abilities. What I'm left with now, though, is an anticlimactic and not terribly rewarding shadow of the former back-to-school season.

Nothing much is expected of me, it seems, but I don't get much in return, either.

We can't go back again to those days of toothless smiles and kitten Trapper Keepers. And while our kids don't need us quite the same way they did back in those days, the fact is we are still needed. So I'm learning to live in this in-between stage, where I'm needed more as a ride and a wallet than the supervisor overseeing the supply list, fundraiser catalog, and the back-to-school event calendar.

The beginning of the school year is just one obvious example of this transition from overseer to facilitator, and I'm working to shift gears. It involves being ready to help when asked while also judging when to interject my advice or feedback when *not* asked. It means being a willing source of funds for necessary expenditures without allowing myself to be treated like a bottomless bank account.

Parenting little ones is active. Hold the hand as you cross the street, teach them how to tie their shoes. But as they get older, our job starts to shift from leader to facilitator, from protector to... patron. And more and more, we wait, in lobbies and school parking lots, by the back door with keys in hand, sitting in the car. By the time they're teenagers, it can start to feel like pretty much the entire job is waiting. For those of us, like me, who prefer to be actively doing, this can be an awkward mindset shift. But waiting is an important part of the job of parenting—sometimes, in the teen years, the most important part.

From speaking up to biting my tongue

When I look back at my early adulthood, I'm alternately amused and terrified by how much I didn't know. We didn't use the word *adulting* back then, but rest assured that I was terrible at it. How was I allowed to navigate the world, knowing so little? I can still clearly remember how unprepared I was for the realities of everything from filing my taxes to scheduling my own dental cleanings.

I wish I'd given myself more license, back then, to not know. I wish I'd leaned on my parents a little more and allowed them to lighten my load a little, as I am sure they gladly would have. But the fact is, I didn't know what I didn't know. As a result, I thought I knew a lot more than I did, and any suggestion to the contrary led only to irritation and indignation on my part. And because I remember that push-pull so well, I try to respect my kids' paths, to stay out of their way when my input isn't asked for.

Parenting older kids means judging which advice or input will really help and which only *seems* like it will help but could instead do harm.

It means learning to differentiate between the things I can fix for them and the things I should let them fix on their own.

It means realizing there are things they may not be able to fix at all, and that it's not my place to barge in with a hammer and nails and start rearranging their lives.

And so often, it means knowing when to speak up and when to bite my tongue.

I don't always get this right—in fact, I could name off four or five examples of having gotten it wrong just in the last month—but in this new and fluctuating state of parenthood, it's always on my mind.

From pursued to pursuer

One day when Clara was four or five years old, she hovered around my vanity, watching me get ready. When I selected a pair of dangly earrings, she dramatically buried her head in my lap and cried, "Noooooooo!"

"What's wrong, honey?" I said to the pitiful little heap of girl draped across my legs.

"Those are your going-out earrings!" she wailed plaintively. And she was right: I wore this particular pair of earrings only when I was leaving the house for the evening. Clara had been watching me anxiously, hoping I'd select a sensible pair of around-the-house

studs or perhaps some grocery-store-ready hoops. But those particular glittery danglies indicated that I was leaving, *without her*—the
last thing in the world she wanted me to do.

My, my, my, how the tables have turned.

As the mother of teenagers and young adults, I'm sometimes
embarrassed by how needy I can feel. Why don't they want to hang
out with me? Why don't they want to do the things I do? Why
don't they like the things I like? I'm always delightfully surprised
when my teens seem to want to spend time with me or show any
appreciation of something I love—and often, in the inverse, disappointed when they disappear for hours at a time or fail to show the
appropriate amount of enthusiasm for an outing I've dreamed up.

These feelings are coming from a couple of different places, I
think. First of all, their aloof disinterest is such a stark contrast to
those arms-full days, in which my children clung to me like weighty
barnacles. Anything I did, they did too–or at least they *hoped* they'd
be invited along.

For another thing, they were so easy to please back then!
Walking around the block, folding the laundry, going to the grocery
store—my offspring were up for any adventure I suggested.

That started to change around adolescence, and there was a
time during each of my kids' teenage years when I truly felt like I
might never spend any willing one-on-one time with them again.
They did all come out of that stage eventually and seem to enjoy
spending time with me again—but I'll never again find a person as
excited to see me, as thrilled to accompany me on literally any task
or outing, as I had when my children were little.

Sometimes it's hard to recognize and accept that my kids will
likely never again bound up to the door like wriggly puppies to jump

all over me when I return home from an outing, that they're not going to cling to my legs to avoid being left behind the moment I open a certain drawer in my jewelry box. And while I now know from experience that it won't last forever, the stage when your teenager shoots down every "fun" idea you suggest can feel awfully deflating.

I have to take a deep breath and remind myself that my teenagers are learning to separate their interests from mine. It's no longer enough of a selling point that I may think something sounds fun; they now need to run it through another series of filters, including what their peers think, what social media is telling them they should think, and what the hormones helping them separate from me and become fully formed adults of their own are telling them to do.

There are, no doubt, other thought processes going on in an adolescence-addled brain that we may not be aware of, things like weighing the chances that they might run into a classmate and die of mortification on the spot. (I've never quite understood why Clara, in particular, finds it humiliating when a peer catches sight of her simply existing outside of school, but apparently it is the most embarrassing thing that can happen.)

It all adds up to a complicated stew of reasons a teenager—no matter how much of an enthusiast of Doing Things, and especially Doing Things with Mom, they might once have been—is likely to deflect, demur, or downright denounce any of my suggestions or make themselves consistently scarce. I try to remind myself that this separation doesn't necessarily mean they don't like me—or, worse, that I have somehow raised inherently boring people who will grow up to be sluggish sofa dwellers with a smartphone permanently attached to their hands—but that it is simply a normal developmental stage like any other.

And though I sometimes want to cling to their legs and beg them to stay like they might have done when I was dangly-earring clad in the old days, I usually manage to pull myself together and not seem too desperate. Nobody wants a Stage-Five Clinger for a mother, after all.

From blazing a trail to letting them lead

When Owen was still undecided about his college choice, the two of us went on a road trip to visit the school I (perhaps not so) secretly hoped he'd choose, Michigan Technological University, or simply "Tech." I'd had big plans for the weekend—to really get acquainted with the city and the school, to hit up the local restaurants, to hang out in the coffee shops and library, to go to a college hockey game. But instead, I got the sickest I'd been in years, with the kind of cold that makes you feel like your head is detached from your body and your body is in fact an uninhabitable place of misery.

Instead of getting to know Owen's new college town as if it were my own, I spent the majority of the weekend in bed and on the sofa. Owen had to learn about the area himself, running out to get me food, taking in the scenery and learning to make sense of what would soon be his college hometown—while I lay on the sofa intermittently coughing and groaning.

Looking back, I think it's best that it played out that way. If I'd been feeling better, it might have been fun to drag Owen to all the places I wanted him to see…but as it was, he got the chance to get to know the area on his own terms, and under his own steam, instead of me dragging him along and living vicariously through his experiences.

At some point, we all have to let go of our parental inclination to blaze a trail and instead let our kids chart their own paths. In my situation, the opportunity was thrust upon me, and I accepted it reluctantly, too buried in a pile of wadded-up tissues to do much about it. But I can see now how with my agenda forced aside and my leadership weakened, Owen was given both the freedom and the incentive to rise to the occasion. It's a lesson I won't soon forget.

From doing for to doing with

Years ago, as my brood grew in number and size and the work of keeping a household running increased, I found myself more and more often hidden away in the kitchen cleaning or in the laundry room folding shirts as the rest of the family hung out. Keeping a household running for a big family is a big job, and I had a lot to *do* in those after-school hours when I had five young kids under my roof.

Perhaps that's how "doing for" became my primary parenting love language.

And most of the time, I was fine with all that doing for. No clean freak by nature, I learned early in motherhood that letting dirt and disorder pile up just meant I had a more demoralizing job to do later. Plus, sequestered in the kitchen, I could think adult thoughts, the din from the living room slightly dampened by the walls between.

Parenting happened in the pauses: I'd finish unloading the dishwasher, then help with homework at the dining-room table, then reload, then help again. I'd chat with the kids about their day while preparing their after-school snack at the island or oversee the emptying of lunch boxes while wiping down counters.

I was available, yes, but also focused on the pile of tasks that defined my day.

In many ways all this doing seemed so much more practical than just hanging out. My kids needed clean clothes, clean dishes, meals; I was equipped to provide those things and quite good at managing it all amid the chaos and noise. There was a routine and an orderly predictability to delivering on those basic needs again and again.

It felt like love in action, and I look back fondly on the time I spent "in service" to my kids when they were little.

I am also aware that things are, by necessity, shifting. To everything there is a season, and as a mother, my "busy season" is winding down, to be replaced by…well, what?

Just as I no longer cut up my teenagers' meat or choose their clothes in the morning, my adult kids don't need or want me to caretake them in the same way I used to. Our relationships sometimes look so different that it feels like I'm starting all over again.

Early motherhood can often give us the impression that we are most valuable for the things we can do for our children. As those kids get older and more competent, it's an opportunity for us to reframe the best way to show up for them. And often, that means simply doing life alongside our grown kids, rather than always giving into the urge to jump in and serve. The switch from simply *being with* my kids instead of always *doing for* them has, I'll admit, been a hard one for me. I keep reminding myself that I'm allowed to enjoy myself, allowed to enjoy my family, allowed to simply exist… even if there *is* still a sink full of dishes in the other room.

LAST CHRISTMAS, AND HOW TO LET GO

When did I cross over the invisible line from hands-full to arms-free? Looking back, I can now see it happened slowly, in stages. For a mother, life is a series of firsts, lasts, and their subcategories: last-firsts and first-lasts. Your youngest child's first tooth: a last-first. Your oldest child's last day of high school: a first-last. Those examples are momentous—and in a way, less momentous, because they are recognizable in the moment they're happening. As I look back, the past decade or so of my life has been absolutely stuffed with the sort of last-firsts and first-lasts that should have triggered my brain to pay attention. And yet, it seemed there were always things to distract me from truly recognizing the gravity of the moment. For example, my oldest child's last day of high school was a momentous occasion to be sure—but the fact that he graduated by the skin of his teeth and my marriage was falling apart at the time short-circuited the celebratory nature of the event.

A few years later, Clara graduated from fifth grade, leaving the same elementary school all four of her younger brothers had gone to and marking the end of my longest and most impactful stage of motherhood. *Look, it's your youngest child's last day of elementary school—this is big,* my mother brain should have warned me. But it was also June of 2020, Clara had been doing her schooling from home for two months, and instead of celebrating a proper last day with all its accompanying ceremony, we drove past a line of teachers, all masked, who handed us Clara's graduation certificate and graded art projects through the window of our car, where we sat—also masked. There were tears in their eyes, and in mine, and a mutual acknowledgment of how wrong this moment felt.

Meanwhile, Clara gathered up her projects and goodbyes with aplomb. By this point, she'd become accustomed to nothing being what she expected. Her eleventh birthday fell on Friday, March 13, 2020, which would also prove to be her last in-person day of elementary school. We got the news that schools would be closing down "for a few weeks" late in the evening of March 12, and I emailed her teacher when I got home. "Is it OK if I send treats to school with Clara tomorrow?" I asked. "I think it'll be OK," her teacher responded. "I just won't pass them out to the other classes." I dropped Clara off the next morning with her Rubbermaid container of brownies, and she did get to have a relatively normal last-ever elementary-school birthday—a small thing for which I'll forever be grateful.

In spring of 2020 my Facebook feed was overtaken by mothers wanting to do things for their kids who were missing out on all the usual milestones: graduation ceremonies, prom, end-of-school-year celebrations. While I don't want to take anything away from the kids, who certainly were missing out, I think it was the mothers who suffered more. *We* knew what was missing, what it meant to us to have those milestones marked, acknowledged, and celebrated. But if the pandemic hadn't happened to remind us of how important those milestones can be, how closely would we have paid attention? Even in the midst of huge change, life is distracting. And sometimes, in order to fully recognize what's happening, you need a moment of reckoning.

And while I've had lots of small reckonings along the way, sometimes a confluence of circumstances all coming together at the same time reminds you that things won't ever be the same again. I experienced one of those confluences the Christmas before last or, as I think of it in my more dramatic and maudlin moments, our last Christmas.

It was 10 a.m. Christmas morning, and I'd been awake for hours. My kids were all still snoozing, long limbs spread with abandon over sofas and guest beds. They'd been up into the wee hours the night before: I saw the messages and photos in our group-text thread when my eyes popped open at 6:30 a.m., even though I'd hoped to sleep 'til eight. I'd tiptoed downstairs and peeked into the living room, wondering if it was time to start setting up for the festivities—but it was clear that there was no reason to hurry. So I started breakfast instead and reflected on just how different things were this year—and how quickly and dramatically they'd be shifting again in the New Year.

Eric—my second husband, whom I met early in the pandemic—and I had gotten married the previous May, and between the location change (Clara, Owen, and I had moved into Eric's house), the fact that Owen was heading off to college the following fall, and the scattering of the three older three boys across the country to new adventures of their own, I knew it was likely this would be the last time that the kids and I would all pile into the house together, just the six of us; the last time we'd play out all our old traditions and insider jokes in the unselfconscious way that's a lot harder to pull off when you've joined your family with another later in life.

Between the divorce, the pandemic, and some personal coming-of-age struggles, my kids' collective exodus from my orbit had previously been slow and stuttered. They left, sure. But they kept on coming back. A big part of that coming back, I know, had been the promise of time spent with siblings. I mean, I'm all right, but I'm also humble enough to know I'm not *that* big of an attraction on my own. Their sibling bonds and family identity have been the main draw that's kept them all hovering around the nest I've built.

But for the first time, that dynamic was about to completely flip. Instead of most of us going about our business on the home front while one or two ventured out into the wider world and then reported back, almost all of them were on the verge of leaving, almost all at once. After years of drifting in and out, suddenly the boys all seemed to be clamoring for the door while Clara and I blinked in confusion.

Clara, who still has two years of high school left after this one, wasn't happy about this turn of events. Over the long run, I hope it'll be good for her to have some space and learn to carve out her own identity separate from "little sister." She'll be doing her own leaping and launching in the next several years, I know, but I appreciate a little quiet space for the two of us to get to spend time together without the constant background hum of her many older brothers.

And then there's me, settling into a new marriage and home, happy for the space to focus a little more tightly inward for a while, while also wondering, *What even happened?*

Things are always changing. I know this. And yet, I notice those changes a lot more during the holidays. That's one of the reasons Christmas can be so sad for so many, I think: it serves as an end-of-year attention-grabber, a milepost that makes us hyperaware of the things done and undone, the passage of time.

Hanging the ornaments on the tree in early December, I couldn't help but remember what my family had been like, what *I* had been like, when I'd taken them down the year before. What we were all like when the ornaments were purchased or, often, made, school photos glued to cardboard and framed in Popsicle sticks. How far we'd come. How much we'd changed. And as I stirred the scrambled eggs that Christmas morning, aware that it could easily be the last, dear God, *the last Christmas morning* when all my kids would wake up under my roof, I fought back the sort of panic one can only feel when it is Christmas morning and one is under the influence of a Bing Crosby binge and the sobby afterglow of *It's A Wonderful Life* and desperately wants to freeze time.

In my twenty-five previous Christmases since becoming a mother, our family had never strayed from our usual routine of stockings-gifts-brunch-lounging, even after the divorce. It had been pretty easy, with most of my kids hovering close to home, and while I'd known all along that it couldn't stay that way forever, waking up for possibly the last time under the same roof as all of my children and only my children and knowing that by the following year things would likely be very different felt like a moment of truth.

I didn't want to give up our usual Christmas routine. I wanted it exactly like it had always been. I wanted to dig in my heels and demand it never change.

But I can't have it all: the growth and flourishing I want for my kids, the freedom and space I need for myself, and a replica of the same holiday until the end of time.

As I toasted the bread and made the tea and got ready to wake the house, as I anticipated watching my family tear eagerly into stockings and wrapping paper, as much as I didn't want those things ever to change, I knew that they would…and needed to. I was ready to have a proper Christmas with my new husband instead of sharing the morning with my ex-husband, as lovely as it was for the kids—and, yes, for ourselves—that we'd managed to keep our old traditions as long as we had. I was ready to create room in my older kids' lives to make space for new ways to celebrate, whether with new friends or partners and, eventually, maybe, their own children.

I hope I'm a part of their future celebrations in some way for as long as I live. But it's time to start passing the baton and bowing out of my role as head magic maker in order to allow them the freedom to do holidays their own way—as well as to create a holiday experience for myself that doesn't rely on them to show up in the same way, year after year, to satisfy my needs.

The truth is, there was always going to be a first time we didn't all gather on Christmas, a first time we didn't do things exactly the same way that we had for the previous quarter century. In spite of my complicated feelings, I knew I had to show up for the Christmas morning that was in front of me, not all the ones that had come before, or the ones that might come after.

So I did what I'd done every Christmas morning for decades: I lined up the stuffed stockings (not without snagging a few chocolates), turned on the tree lights, fired up the classic Christmas playlist, and called out my merriest "Merry Christmas!" Watching them all together, I reveled in it, laughing and teary at turns.

At some point, surrounded by paper and ribbon and candy wrappers and balled-up socks, I couldn't wait for the clamor to be over, to retreat to my bedroom with a mimosa and a magazine. Yet I also knew I'd never really be ready for it to end. That's motherhood in a nutshell, I suppose, and maybe Christmas is just the densest, most concentrated version of what's in the nut.

Perhaps some of the sadness over facing the "last" of any of these big events is the knowledge that we're out of chances to appreciate it enough, to really notice every moment, to get it exactly right. And one of the hardest lessons I've learned as a mother is that not only will I not ever get it exactly right, I probably won't remember it later even when I do.

YOU WON'T REMEMBER THIS LATER

I have a specific memory, from when Jacob was a baby, of a little game I'd play while he was lying alongside me. I'd stretch out his little legs and then, with my hand, mark the spot on my body where his foot stopped, and I'd note how much farther down my leg his feet reached than the last time I'd noticed.

At first, I remember feeling excited and gratified by Jacob's rapid lengthening, evidence of his miraculous personhood. It was still mind-blowing to me that this human I'd created with my body was now here, continuing to grow on the *outside* of my body. Yes, I provided the milk and warmth, but his cells did the rest, independent of my body's machinery. What a wonder.

But when his body reached halfway from my armpit to my knees, the tenor of the "game" turned from celebratory to something a little more somber. Instead of excitedly measuring in anticipation of more growth, I began to be reminded of just how quickly time was passing. The "game" became a sort of melancholy watch: I used his continuing length as a reminder to myself to live in the present by appreciating, noticing, and remembering each precious day of his baby life, and when I think back, I can remember with surprising clarity just what it felt like to be the young mother of baby Jacob.

At least…I *think* it was Jacob.

One thing is certain: I *definitely* measured the length of some baby or other next to mine, marking how far *someone's* chubby little toes reached on my side this week and then the next and the next. But now that I think about it more carefully, maybe Isaac was the babe-in-arms when I began playing this little game. Or Will? Maybe I did it with more than one of my babies. Or all five? Maybe I only did it once and thought about doing it again later and never did, but my brain filled in the blank spots, as it has a habit of doing. I sometimes wonder, *Did any of this really happen?*

Truthfully, I'm pretty positive that I did this first (and often) with Jacob, and I'm sure I did it at least a handful of times with each of the other kids. But I share this fuzzy memory, and my own self-doubt about it, to raise this point: if you're a parent of younger kids right now, you are probably not going to remember this (whatever "this" may be) later, despite your best intentions. And if you're a parent of older kids and can't quite put your finger on which kid did what in your older motherhood memories, or you are having a hard time conjuring up many specific memories at all, join the club.

We love to tell parents to slow down, to pay attention, to savor the little moments. I definitely tried to be intentional about this when my kids were younger, with the mistaken idea that forced and effortful "noticing" would somehow slow down the process of my kids' getting bigger—if not in actuality, then at least in my perception.

But I was wrong. You can notice every little moment with all your might, and those moments will still pass incredibly, unreasonably quickly. And the real kicker is that no matter how hard you try to lock it all into your memory, later you inevitably find that so much has been forgotten.

If this sounds familiar, it's not because you have a particularly poor memory or you were any worse than the rest of us at "slowing down and noticing." It's more that motherhood itself induces a sort of amnesia. The jumble of monotonous and magical moments all tangled together, the long, long days and impossibly short years, all tinged by sleep deprivation: it's not a particularly reliable recipe for even passable recall.

When I look at photos of my kids from that stage of parenthood, I'm often momentarily surprised. Oh, that's what they looked like? And wait, that's what *I* looked like? (Why didn't anyone give it to me straight during the era of the *Kate + Eight* haircut?)

The further I get from those days, the more I need photographic evidence to remind myself of the way it was, the way I was, the way we all were.

Babyhood memories are foggy. Certain things stand out, of course: Jacob's first haircut, Isaac's first words, Will's fist closed around his cake at his first birthday. Owen's tentative pride at preschool drop-off; long, leisurely afternoons at the park with Clara once all her brothers were in school. And I can remember a lot of our surroundings vividly, too: the apartments and homes we lived in, the cars I drove, sometimes down to the doorknobs and upholstery. I have an uncannily specific memory of the car seat my two oldest boys used as toddlers, the way the copious Cheerios crumbs contrasted with its navy-blue liner.

But for the most part, the details of our lives together through the years are hazy and nondescript—less like many days put together with five specific and individual children and more like one very long, very repetitive day with a rotating cast of little ones whose faces I can barely make out.

Is it because I didn't pay attention, or simply because it was a long time ago and because, well, raising small children tends to be repetitive and not particularly memorable?

I remember that, in those quiet moments after they'd fallen asleep nursing and I'd lie there trying to decide whether to move them or just stay there and read while they finished out a nap, I would remind myself, "This is fleeting. This won't last. Soon those bent-up legs and tiny toes will reach to your knees. Notice it, savor it, appreciate it." Interestingly, I remember the thought of reminding myself to notice *more than I actually remember the thing I was working so hard to notice.*

No matter how much noticing and savoring and appreciating I did, the time still marched on, and I still can't go back. Not only that, but I can't exactly conjure up lazy naptime memories specific to each child, either. It's more of a general memory: there's a bed, and a fuzzy head tucked under my arm, and perhaps a little dribble of milk running down a soft cheek. It's all my babies at once and no baby in particular.

Maybe savoring isn't about slowing down the time or remembering every tiny detail as though it just happened: in retrospect, it seems impossible to manipulate our fickle and inconsistent memories to that degree. Maybe it's not about remembering more clearly down the road, because no matter how hard we tried to lock in memories, my actual memories (and lack thereof) have taught me that their accurate recall, regardless of how precious they felt in the moment, is never guaranteed.

All of life involves forgetting what happened yesterday, and last year, and last decade. All memories are eventually lost, whether through the simple human act of forgetting or the more dramatic effects of dementia or even death. Maybe noticing and appreciating are simply about making *this* moment better, and the next, and the next...whether or not the moments stay with us in the future or slip away quietly without taking leave.

I like to believe that somewhere, locked away in my subconscious memory, are the specific memories I can't seem to conjure up no matter how hard I try. The second time something momentous happened, along with the first. The days we did nothing in particular alongside the vacations and holidays and birthdays. And I like to believe that those memories will live on as I get older and, more and more, my brain shoves them aside to make room for new data. That no matter the reason those memories may fade into the background or become hard to access, they still exist somewhere, like files in a cabinet stored in the attic.

But whether or not that's true, this is: Life is happening right now. My boys are now men. My girl is nearly a woman. We are not always together. And yet, right now, we are still here. I don't have the promise of memories tomorrow, but I have today.

I cringe when I think I may be perceived as the kind of mom who can't help reminding newer moms, "Hug your babies" and "It'll be over before you know it" and "One day, you'll look back and..."

Those moms may be seasoned, but they're forgetful, too: they've forgotten what it's like to know all that in your bones while also feeling like the days are crawling by so slowly that some moments are almost unbearable.

So please believe me: I'm not reminding other moms that they'll forget because I'm sitting high on some perch, smugly applauding myself for appreciating every moment. I'm saying it because I'm still walloped and whiplashed by the realization of how fast time flies. I'm saying it because I still wake up in the middle of the night in a sort of existential dread about the passage of time and the disappearance of my littles, many years after most of them were, in fact, little. I'm saying it because, even knowing all that, I will still fail to adequately appreciate the presence of the present.

Twenty-seven years into motherhood, even after the intense cadence of early motherhood has given way to a different sort of pace, I still need the reminder—and the reassurance—that no matter which stage of the ride we're in, we're all just hanging on for dear life most of the time, showing up as best we know how, appreciating as best we can…and poring over photos later to remind ourselves that it all happened and we were there.

FOUR QUICK REMINDERS FOR WHEN YOU JUST CAN'T REMEMBER:

1. **Focus on feelings.**
   Even if you were a careful baby-book documenter (and if you're anything like me, you…*were not*), information has a way of getting lost over time. Luckily, I've found that even when I can't remember exactly *what* happened in a particular scenario (e.g.,

which word was a specific child's first or the exact age at which they took their first step), I can often still remember how I *felt* when it happened. The emotions, and other details like setting and time of year, are very often easier to recall—and may matter even more than the actual facts.

2. **Keep things in historical perspective.**

We've been raising kids in an era where every moment of their lives can be not only recorded and documented, but also shared—instantly. It's helpful, I think, to remember that this is a very new phenomenon. There's a meme that says something to the effect of "I took more photos of my kids yesterday than my parents took of me in my entire childhood," and that pretty well sums it up, I think. My childhood photo albums were filled with just a handful of pictures of special events, trips, and holidays and barely any of the ordinary days between. Go back a generation, to my mother's childhood, and there are even fewer photos to document her family's life. One more generation back, in my grandmother's childhood, family photos were a very rare and precious thing. Those kids were just as loved, their childhoods just as real, their memories just as sacred.

3. **Ask your kids about *their* memories.**

No one ever said that mothers have to be the sole gatekeepers of family memories. What kids remember is fascinating, and what's even more fascinating is how their memory of a situation can differ so much from my own memory of the same situation. And yet, who's to say my memory is more accurate than theirs or that a photo or journal entry would have set the record straight? Memories are subjective and changeable things.

4. **It's not too late.**

This one's for the moms with boxes of twenty-year-old photos still waiting to be organized and half-empty baby books you would still love to finish. If memory keeping in the form of scrapbooking, journaling, or even simple photo box or album organizing has been elusive so far, take a deep breath and dive in. Sign up for the scrapbooking workshop, purchase the service that promises to help you make sense of your thousands of digital photos, scrawl your best guesses in the empty spots in the baby books, or simply get the boxes of memorabilia out on your next free Saturday morning, dig in, and see what you've got. Even if the moments are years or decades in the past, it's still worth your time and effort to wrangle them. You still have time, and there's no time like the present.

THE "MUSCLE MEMORY" OF MOTHERHOOD, AND WHAT I LEARNED AT THE MALL

When my first two kids, Jacob and Isaac, were tiny, we logged many, *many* hours at the mall. As I pushed a double stroller past Banana Republic and through Macy's, my weekly visit was an easy way to move my body during bitter Michigan winters, and the window displays gave contours and color to long hours spent with tiny children. Strawberry smoothies from Orange Julius and Auntie Anne's pretzels dipped in melted cheese became the flavors of my early motherhood.

But at some point early on, the retail rose lost its bloom. I can't exactly remember when or why: maybe it was one too many mid-Victoria's Secret outbursts from my spirited second child. Or perhaps it was the addition of a third baby and the realization that I no longer had enough arms to push the double stroller *and* keep one of the kids from pawing the scantily clad mannequins that was the straw that broke this mom's mall-loving back.

All I remember is that, rather abruptly, shopping for leisure stopped being fun—or even, typically, tolerable—with children in tow.

So I stopped going...for the better part of two decades.

Sure, I popped into malls on my own every now and then, when I could get away without my children, but I went a very long time without bringing my children into any indoor retail establishment featuring multiple shops. And once I saw how much easier shopping was without kids in tow, I avoided bringing them on even quicker trips: the grocery store, the hardware store, even—gasp—Target. The kids got bigger—even growing all the way up, some of them—and yet, my anticipatory stress level when considering a family shopping trip lingered.

I chalk up my extended mall aversion to an experience I call the "muscle memory" of motherhood, kind of a cross between the unconscious motor actions we learn to perform without thinking about them and the way high-stress mothering experiences can turn themselves into anticipatory reactions over time.

When our kids are small, over time our brains become attuned to potential dangers, and our bodies respond to that potential danger. But even now, long after it's stopped being necessary, I reflexively push cups away from the edge of the table, out of the reach of curious little fingers; I swing my hips from side to side as I stand, years after my youngest became too big to hold.

If you're like me, you started thinking differently in those early motherhood years, too. You began proactively anticipating potential hassles or disruptions to efficiency, and you got used to running each decision through a series of superquick mental filters: Will this event interfere with naptime? Will the venue be too crowded for a stroller? How many diapers do I need to bring? Will there be food my kid will eat?

More than using just your eyes and ears, you learned to rely on extrasensory perception. A potential need anticipated? The nearly imperceptible shift in a room's energy, telling you an inhabitant is thirsty or hungry, bored, irritated, or sad? If you're like me, your mom muscle memory urged—and still urges—you to jump into action at the merest whiff of need: refilling plates and glasses, giving hugs or encouragement, asking open-ended questions, changing the channel.

Bless our hard-working brains for doing that work for us, right? For years those easy, habitable routes helped us avoid missed naps and meltdowns and this-isn't-worth-the-trouble situations. They helped us put our baser instincts aside to prioritize our kids' safety and flourishing. I'd argue, in fact, that muscle memory is part of what helps make us "good" moms. Over the twenty-seven years I've been a mom, my neural pathways have carved so many helpful grooves for me, and I'm truly grateful for them.

But here's the problem: the very same neural pathways that helped create my mom muscle memory haven't always kept up with the times.

As my kids grew, my learned responses to those old, old triggers didn't always respond to my new reality. Those old messages, old experiences, old stories wired themselves firmly into my neural pathways, so that even when I wasn't consciously aware of it, I was still always thinking, always planning, always tightening my jaw in anticipation of disaster at all times—even when the actual danger of that particular disaster was as out-of-date as my 1997 maternity wardrobe.

The downside of all this preemptive self-protection is this: we avoid experiences that could be easy, enriching, or just plain fun, because our old wiring tells us there might be a tantrum or a sibling squabble or the consequences of a missed bedtime to deal with.

Or maybe we find ourselves reflexively turning to coping mechanisms we no longer need. Ever found yourself reaching for a 5 p.m. glass of wine to counteract the mania of a "witching hour" that hasn't existed in years?

No judgment here—just before dinnertime, a house full of young kids can be so overwhelming that it's natural to want to retreat, zone out, numb yourself. But suddenly you realize you're drinking alone in a quiet kitchen in anticipation of a frenzy that hasn't happened in close to a decade. On closer reflection you may realize that what you *really* crave is connection with the teenagers who now silently retreat to their bedrooms and that your old standby crutch is neither necessary nor helpful in your getting what you need. Trust me on this one.

Which brings me back to the mall. The truth is this: just like making dinner for my family right now, taking my two youngest to the mall no longer even remotely resembles what that experience would have been like ten or fifteen years ago. So why waste so much mental energy digging in on ancient experiences to justify my dogged avoidance of it?

A couple summers ago I took Clara and Owen—then thirteen

and sixteen—to the mall for the first time in a very long time. Owen needed hours behind the wheel for driver's ed, Clara needed a few shirts for her back-to-school wardrobe, and the more I thought about it, the more I found myself in desperate need of an Auntie Anne's pretzel with cheese.

Clara, Owen, and I started in my safe place, Barnes & Noble, where I meandered around the self-help and fiction sections while the kids hung out by the Manga. Finally, when I'd worked up the gumption to enter the mall's interior, Owen and Clara browsed a few teenage clothes stores, and I took a leisurely stroll through Victoria's Secret. (The lingerie section is a lot less embarrassing to navigate without a three-year-old boy trying to feel up the mannequins, friends.) Later, as I sipped a leisurely tea in the café, Owen and Clara—get this—*went and bought me a pretzel and brought it to me.*

And I realized something that day: the mall is actually the perfect place to hang out with your teenagers. There's something there for everyone. It allows for low-stakes independence for the kids and bra- or book-browsing time for you. Also, there are pretzels. With cheese. No, it wasn't the most culturally enriching way to spend an evening with my kids, but you know what? As a lazy weekday evening goes, it wasn't a bad way to spend some time, either. No wonder that, back in the '90s, my parents took me to the mall nearly every weekend.

Adjusting to our new reality isn't always easy or quick. And rewiring our brains doesn't always happen automatically. Often— sometimes *many times daily*—I find myself anticipating a reality that no longer exists. What follows are some of the ways that old reality shows up for moms in this stage (and how to adjust our outdated thinking).

We help people who don't need helping.

Ever find yourself jumping up to refill a plate for a perfectly capable teenager or "helping" a young adult out of a simple jam when they didn't even ask for your assistance? Yeah, me too.

One of the challenges of this transitional stage of parenting is recognizing that the things our kids needed from us five or ten or fifteen years ago aren't necessarily the same things they need now. In fact, they may exude a bravado that implies they *don't need anything from us at all*. And somehow, we need to keep that from breaking our hearts while recognizing that our value comes from a much deeper source than the well of "What can Mom do for me today?"

Over the years our kids became accustomed to drawing from that well, but now they're off looking for their own sources of water. And our task becomes a daily self-reminder that *we are not the well*. We never were.

Look, I'm a natural nurturer, and sometimes I really enjoy refilling milk glasses and dishing out seconds. But just as often, those built-in urges are based on outdated information about what my kids need from me or what makes me valuable to my family—or just valuable, *as a human being*.

It took me some time to recognize that this process of resetting my boundaries, restraining from jumping in, and reinforcing my sense of self-worth is a "me" problem, not a "them" problem. By establishing their independence and breaking away, my kids are just doing their jobs. My job is just as necessary, and just as developmentally appropriate: I'm working to figure out who I am, what they really need from me, and, perhaps more important, what I need from myself.

We stress out over situations that aren't stressy.

At some point along the way, your body and brain probably came to the understanding that taking little kids to a busy mall, or the fair, or a parade, really sucks—so you looked for ways to avoid the experience. Or, you got stressed out by the possibility of crowds, or parties, or restaurants with complicated menus. You had a bad experience trying to get your baby to sleep in a hotel, or listening to a screaming toddler on the interstate, so now planning a family road trip sounds like a horror show. Or you got used to protecting your family dinners at home, to the point that outside invitations or events felt like a violent intrusion.

And you didn't just learn *what to avoid*; you also learned *when to act*. A thud from an upstairs bedroom, a scream, the singularly terrifying sound of a full-stomached retch: all these sounds could throw your body into adrenaline-fueled action mode.

However different your circumstances now, I bet some of the residue of those early Situational Scaries is still with you. It's worth considering the following questions: How is that old wiring showing up in the way I plan events now? What have I been saying "no" to reflexively, and could I begin to consider saying "yes" instead, even if just now and then? Am I carrying around anticipatory tension that I don't need to hold on to anymore?

We turn to counterproductive coping crutches.

Remember my comment about the witching-hour wine a few paragraphs back? For all our recent discussion about "mommy wine culture," it seems that some of the experts who tsk-tsk over maternal alcohol consumption often fail to acknowledge how exhausting evenings at home with small children can be.

Moms typically find ourselves in the position of homework management, clutter control, behavior modification, and dinner preparation—all at the same time. And when you have small kids, it's not just intense—it can feel impossible.

When I had five children under twelve, sitting down to dinner with them all resembled a goat square dance around a blazing dumpster fire. Occasionally amusing, and usually worth the hassle…but also stressful, smelly, messy, and time-consuming. For years I had to psych myself up during the dinner hour, trying to inject little moments of joy or pleasure or at least purpose into the pedestrian task of cooking up a pan of ziti or a pot roast while breaking up scrimmages in the next room over, all without letting my kids have too much screen time.

Hence the 5 p.m. heavy pour (or two, if I'm honest). And I'm not going to say a word of judgment if you also found yourself in that situation on the regular.

But a few years ago, I realized that I was still carrying the latent stress from those early days into my experience of putting dinner on the table now—even though everything about pulling together dinner for a much smaller family of older kids had completely changed. I suddenly realized: I'm trying to hide from a situation that's not even scary! And it opened up so much space for healthier new habits.

Turns out, numbing myself in today's version of dinnertime isn't just unnecessary, it's counterproductive. As my kids pull away and seek their own independence, I want *more* time with them, not less, and I want to be as present as I can for every moment.

I'm certainly not going to say that I never enjoy a glass of wine while I'm making dinner anymore, but the intent around it has completely changed (and the amount has naturally modified as a result).

It's been a long time since a kid ran around my dinner table with a diaper on his head. There's just nothing to hide from anymore, and everything to show up for.

Maybe your coping mechanism of choice is scrolling Instagram, shopping, or snarfing down cookies in the pantry. Many of us have compulsions and addictions, and they often grow slowly and gradually from small actions we take to help us get through the day. Overcoming them may require a mix of strategies, from mindfulness practices to support from others to, sometimes, professional help. But the first step may be asking yourself, in the moment: Which reality am I escaping from? And is that "reality" even…real?

FIVE WAYS TO REWIRE YOUR "MOM MUSCLE MEMORY"

Whether we're reacting to stress that doesn't really exist or jumping up to help capable kids, rewiring old thought patterns can take time and repetition. Here are some strategies that can help.

1. Ask yourself: Is this true?

Through yoga I've learned how to practice separating what's actually happening from my perception of it—which is typically clouded by assumptions of what might happen in the future or by memories of what I've experienced in the past. One of the ways I do this is by simply asking myself, "Is this true?" anytime my brain starts trying to get my body to react to its version of reality. This is a great practice to put into effect when you feel your jaw clenching in anticipation of an upcoming event. Notice how your body feels and which story your brain is trying to tell it, and then check in with reality. Is anything stressful actually happening, or are old narratives getting your body all whipped up into fight-or-flight mode? What is the true story of what's happening right now?

2. Breathe and be in the moment.

The antidote to the habit of getting stuck in the past—or its equally unhelpful cousin, the tendency to jump ahead to an unknown future—is to really immerse ourselves in the reality of right-where-we-are. Taking a few moments to breathe and notice the space. Next time you feel your jaw clenching or fists balling up in anticipation of stress, take a moment to notice what's really going on. How does that anticipation feel inside your body? Where is it coming from?

3. Let your kids be who they are today.

Our children grow up so fast—but it also happens at a nearly imperceptible pace, right in front of our eyes. How can both of these things be true? I don't know, but this fast yet slow pace can really scramble my ability to keep up with what's happening. I often miss when my kids have developed the ability to handle new responsibilities or freedoms. Or, conversely, I've sometimes overestimated their ability to handle things like the complicated social pressures they face or their willingness to talk to me when they have a problem (just because they did when they were five doesn't mean they will at fifteen, after all).

So I try to let my kids be exactly who they are, right now. I still set boundaries and limits, encourage them and challenge them—but with the understanding of what their capabilities are today, not what they were yesterday, or what they might be tomorrow, or what their peers appear to be capable of.

It's one of the hardest things I've ever done as a mother, and I often mess it up. But letting our kids be who they are today is an effort worth showing up for again and again.

4. **Give yourself grace.**

Yes, your kids may be clutched in the ravages of adolescence, and that explains their occasionally irrational behavior—but have you tried considering what *your* body and brain and heart and soul are going through right now? You're on the precipice of a massive identity shift, your body and face are changing, and your hormones are probably going just as off the rails as any teenage girl's. Give yourself a break. Many breaks. All. The. Breaks.

You're working so hard, developing new coping skills, patience, and perspective all the time. You're learning and growing and becoming. Don't allow that one time you flew off the handle at the dishes piled up in the sink, or martyred yourself on a family vacation only to feel resentful later, to be the narrative that defines you as a mother or human being in the future.

5. **Keep the long view in mind.**

Since my kids were little, I've continually reminded myself that I'm parenting for the long view. Over the years that's meant putting my kids' character development over contemporary cultural external markers of success like academics and awards. It's meant prioritizing our relationships—both between me and each of my kids, between my kids and their siblings, and between all of us as a family unit—over onetime behavioral outcomes. This has never been easy, but it's more worth it than ever now that we're standing on the edge of whatever our we're-all-adults-here relationships will look like. I try to see moments of tension and uncertainty as opportunities to help shape what I want those relationships to look like in the future, while also reminding myself that there is a whole life out there for me outside of what the past two and a half decades have looked like—decades of life for me in which "Mom" is not my primary identity.

Those mental grooves that helped us simply get by when our kids were really little became deep and well worn over time. Our brains learned to take shortcuts just to help us survive. But if you're like me, you're ready for a new definition of living that leaves room for openness, adventure, and ease instead of the clenched-fist narratives of "We can't," "I must," and "This is going to be hard." Let's unfurl our grip around those earlier limitations and embrace a bigger idea of what's possible. There's a big, broad life on the other side—even if it does sometimes start as small as a trip to the mall.

THE LONELIEST YEARS

During a talk I gave at my church a few months ago, I mentioned that I was writing a book about parenting older kids. Though it wasn't a major thrust of the talk, in the lobby afterward I was flanked by mothers, all with the same hungry look in their eyes, telling me their stories. The feeling I came away with: the experience of parenting young adults was completely different from what these women expected, and—here's the kicker—*they don't feel they have anyone they can talk to about it.*

While it's become more acknowledged—in certain circles anyway—just how isolating motherhood can be, we tend to reserve that recognition for new moms who've been freshly thrust into a brand-new reality they know little about, buried under piles of diapers and mauled by sticky fingers, often with no support system in sight. And of course, I know from hard-earned experience how real that brand of loneliness can be. I'd never discount the isolation and lack of support that can make new motherhood so much more difficult than it needs to be.

Yet I've noticed that the loneliness inherent to parenting older kids doesn't get nearly the same level of attention, even though in some ways it can be even more crushing.

Maybe that's because we don't see it. After all, once our kids are old enough that we can start leaving the house in regular intervals again, what's stopping us from connecting with others? Nights or weekends away with friends, time spent pursuing hobbies, date nights with our partners: yes, admittedly, all are easier to pull off when we're no longer in the arms-full stage of parenting.

But while the amount of time we're able to spend out in the world may increase dramatically, *that doesn't automatically inoculate us against loneliness.* As kids get older we're able to get out and around other adult people more. But it's also likely the people we're around don't know what's *really* going on in our hearts and homes.

It's amazing, actually, how terribly lonely it's possible to feel while surrounded by other people—and in my experience, there's a particularly bitter flavor of loneliness that often accompanies the experience of parenting teens and young adults. The feeling of isolation doesn't necessarily flee in this stage; it just goes underground.

Maybe the loneliness we feel stems from the fact that it seems so much harder to be open about what's happening with our kids as they grow than it was when they were little. Parenting small kids is absolutely a stressful experience, but as we discussed in the last chapter, it's often also a communal (and certainly a public) one. When I was the mom whose preschooler was melting down at the supermarket, or whose toddler babbled loudly during a church service, I'd get supportive smiles and knowing winks all around. "We've been there, too," those looks seemed to say, and I shored up under the support even as I shrank under the glare of the naysayers.

While there are always exceptions, I think this is a pretty common experience. Cranks and grumps aside, for the most part people give little kids a pass for their normal developmental foibles, understanding that small children do, well, *what small children do*. Everyone knows what to expect from babies and toddlers and preschoolers, it seems: they push boundaries and test limits and express their small-kid-ness—and much of the time, if it looks like you're trying at all, the other adults around you will understand and give you a pass.

And even if the people around you are grumpy and judgmental and you're in a hot-cheeked flush of embarrassed agony over your kid's antics, well, it's all out there in public. Whether they like it or not, everyone else in the room is in this moment with you—and even if you can't bear to lift your head and look around, in every face-flushed moment of motherly mortification, there's likely another parent sending you a silent look of support.

But at some point, those public displays of societal smile-and-nod "I've been there" solidarity start to fade as parenting goes slowly underground. Ask any parent whose child is struggling with substance abuse, or flunking out of high school, or experiencing depression, or who has gotten in serious trouble at school: while these problems are still technically "normal," and even relatable, there's nothing *cute* about them—and they're likely to be mostly playing out in private, inside the four walls of a family home.

This change begins when your kids reach elementary-school age. By the time they're teenagers acting up, goofing off, and expressing their teenager-ness, there's no "pass" left for them...or for you. And young adults? Forget it. If they haven't figured out how to be fully adulting members of society by twenty-two, they're clearly doomed...and it probably seems like it's all your fault.

There's so much I could say here about how we've found ourselves in this situation to begin with. How young people have been stripped of meaningful rites of passage, the structure of community, and the security of following a well-laid path while the expectations of "success" have constantly risen while their achievability plummets. How parents have absorbed all the demands and responsibilities of helping to launch young people into the world with very little social support—but plenty of judgment and criticism.

We'll get to that later, friends. But right now I want to talk about the loneliness we feel when we find ourselves in a stage of motherhood that was intended to be a communal experience but has instead become an often painful, shameful, and, most of all, *private* affair. It shouldn't be this way, and yet, it makes total sense that we've gotten to this point.

In our current culture of knee-jerk, drive-by critiques and "zero-tolerance" hot takes, letting others have a peek inside your family's private dynamics is an incredibly vulnerable and scary thing. If you vent, you may feel embarrassed, self-conscious, or even angry at or disgusted with your child. If you share something big that's going on, it's possible you'll find yourself on the defensive, trying to justify the parenting choices you made long ago that seem to have led to a less-than-ideal result, or making a case for how you're dealing with the issue now.

Unhelpful, judgmental responses or even well-meaning advice may make you doubt yourself even more. And then there's the additional obstacle: sharing at all can feel like it's violating your child's privacy and their trust in you, which may already be on rocky ground to begin with.

It seems easier, doesn't it, to just slap a smile on and pretend everything is great? No wonder so many of us don't talk about what's going on at all.

And yet, we *need* to be talking to one another, not only because our struggles can feel like too much to bear alone, but also because sharing them with one another is the only way we will see how truly relatable they are.

Many of us become masters of disguise in this stage of parenting, too afraid of the judgment, alienation, or even well-meaning sympathy we might face to be honest about what's really going on in our families. But I promise you, whatever your young person or your entire family is dealing with, there are other parents in your community—maybe even on your block—who are in the same boat. Depression, addiction, a general lack of direction—these are all-too-common struggles in today's young people, and no matter what you're going through in your family, you are not alone.

I can't solve our current gaps in social support in this book, but I *can* offer some advice—including a few things I'd do differently when dealing with some of my own kids' developmental doozies—to help you navigate these issues while still feeling solid support beneath your feet.

Find groups specific to your struggles.

Not all support is created equal. While open ears and hearts can encourage you no matter who they belong to, it can be life-changing to encounter more specific encouragement from other parents who've walked the same path as yours. If your child is dealing with a specific, acute struggle, try googling resources for parents in the same boat—and then take the crucial step of reaching out. Whether asking for advice anonymously online or mustering up the courage to connect in person with other parents in your situation, you might be surprised at how much relief you feel in simply being "seen" by another parent who understands what you're going through.

Don't let anyone make you doubt what you know to be true about your kid.

I've always lived by the general rule that I don't badmouth my kids to other people. Sure, I engage in a good-natured "Kids these days!"–style conversation with my best pals, and we swap plenty of exasperating stories, but we typically balance them with recognition of our kids' strengths and successes, and an undercurrent of shared recognition that our offspring are really pretty great people.

I'm fortunate that most of the people in my inner circles share a desire to build up the young people in our lives—including one another's kids—rather than tear them down. So it has always caught me off guard when I encounter another sort of person: those who jump to believe the worst about my kids, their own kids, *any* kids, really. And even the people who are typically cheerleaders for my kids can take on a decidedly more negative tone at times if they're personally triggered by what my kid is going through or they have strong "In my day…" views without a lot of personal experience to back it up.

I'm not proud to admit I've occasionally let those hot-take

opinions color what I believe about my own children and the situation at hand, particularly when we've been dealing with a difficult dynamic or even a major crisis.

Now, as my kids' mother, I know I am sometimes guilty of attaching my rose-colored glasses a bit too firmly to the bridge of my nose. My offspring are far from perfect, and I occasionally can benefit from being reminded when they are behaving badly.

But while it's one thing to have a friend lovingly point out that my child is likely taking advantage of my generosity or seems to be struggling with a mental health issue I can't fix, it's another thing to have someone tell you your child is selfish, lazy, delusional, or crazy. And when you're in the vulnerable place of being disappointed by, frustrated with, or afraid for your young person, absorbing that negativity can have the destructive effect of making you lose sight of what you know to be true about your child and your family, and it can derail you from your big-picture relationship goals.

In moments of weakness, it's normal to let an outsider's assessment of what's happening in your family temporarily color what your intuition is telling you is actually true. Here are some ways I've found to work through those assessments in order to discern the truth:

→ First, I conduct a reality check. Is it possible I read ill intent into loving honesty? Was there any wisdom to be gleaned from the conversation, even the parts that put me on the defensive—and if so, what action can I take?

→ I think it's also really helpful to get another perspective from someone whose bias is more likely to be a blend of loving and truthful. You likely have people in your life who know and

appreciate your kid but who will give it to you straight: a favorite coach, teacher, or boss; a longtime pastor or family friend;
your coparent or a sibling.

→ Finally, I find it helpful to remind myself what I know to be
true. Eric taught me this little trick early in our relationship,
and I've found it incredibly helpful in times when emotions like
defensiveness or frustration are playing tricks with my mind.
Ask yourself: What do you know to be true about your child,
yourself, your family?

Sometimes I've come away from conversations that felt like
rampant bashing of my kid only to realize that the other person
had some good, honest, and even accurate feedback—and that
perspective can have value, even if it was delivered less tactfully than
I would have preferred. Other times, when I look back at a conversation, I realize the other person was operating from a position of
having an ax to grind about modern-day parenting, outdated ideas
about what should be expected of young adults, and/or an outsize
memory of their own responsibility level and work ethic at said kid's
age. When I go through the three steps above, it becomes much
easier to identify the nugget of truth (if there was one), reorient
myself with what's really true, let the rest go…and then refer to the
following two tips.

Share, but self-protect.

It's a sad but incontrovertible fact that not everyone in your inner
circle is going to be the right person to talk to about what's going
on in your family. We all bring our own upbringing, experiences,

expectations, and biases to our relationships, and I've found that sometimes the people I hope will be able to provide the right kind of support in a specific situation simply can't. It doesn't necessarily mean the relationship isn't as close as I thought, only that we are coming from such different places that their advice or perspective creates confusion or harm rather than confidence and help.

My personal litmus test: if I constantly feel on the defensive while discussing my kid with a specific person—if they seem dismissive of my concerns or critical of my parenting, if they speak harshly about my child in a way that seems over-the-top or inaccurate, or if they persist in telling me what they would do in my situation (I promise, *they have no idea what they would do in my situation*) or in giving advice that my gut tells me misses the mark—I will shift future mentions of that child to only positive, vague, "just the facts" updates and quickly change the subject when questions are asked.

Remember, whatever we choose to share about our children is up to us. We can share because it helps us feel better and less alone. We can share because we need advice or an outsider's perspective. Or, we can share because we feel the other person is in a position to help us, or our child, cope with what's going on. But we don't ever *owe* it to anyone to share what's happening with our kid *just because they asked*, even if that person is a close friend or family member. Save your most private sharing for confidants who give solid advice, offer real help, and, most of all, increase your sense of peace and confidence.

And keep an open mind: in the end, you may be surprised at who those people turn out to be.

Watch what you say about other people's kids.

Creating an environment of trust is a two-way street. Hey, I'm only human: occasionally I participate in a little schadenfreude-laced "Can you believe what so-and-so's kid did?" gossip with my besties—particularly when the "so-and-so" in question is a queen of sanctimony. But I very often regret it afterward. The way I see it, any judgment I lob toward some child whose mother *isn't* in the room could also apply to a child whose mother *is* in the room—either right now or sometime in the future. It could be one of my best friends' kids; maybe one day it'll be *my* kid.

Now, again, I'm only human, and I'm not promising I'll never discuss other people's struggles with my friends. I read a theory recently that states that gossip may serve an evolutionary purpose, helping us to bond and protect ourselves from the future bad behavior of others. I think there's a lot of value in keeping other community members aware of what's happening around us and analyzing community drama with the people we trust most. I just try to approach these topics with fairness and kindness when they come up—because, gosh, I'd really hope others would do the same for me, and also because I think it helps create an environment where moms can be more honest and forthright about what's happening in their families and homes without fearing the immediate judgment or alienation of other parents.

If I want people in my life with whom I can trust my family's hardest moments, I need to be a person other people can trust with theirs. I try to keep that reminder in mind when I'm tempted to indulge in a particularly mean-spirited tea-spilling session.

It will almost certainly take some effort and a fair amount

of trial and error to surround yourself with people who help you (and your children) feel seen, not judged. Our society is not set up to support families through the entire parenting process—a big problem that I can't adequately tackle in this book.

But none of us, at any stage of parenting, are actually going through this alone...and maybe, if we keep sharing what's happening in our own lives, we'll be able to remember that fact.

THE TRUTH ABOUT THE EMPTY NEST

Our home is perched at the top of a hill, overlooking a field with a pond that's a popular watering spot for local wildlife. Depending on the time of year, I might see ten or fifteen turkey meandering around the yard and a dozen or more deer cross through our yard on a typical day.

In the spring, you don't see fawns very often. This is usually what's called their "bed phase," where a newborn fawn will be stashed in a safe place by its mother, who returns only for brief visits. Later, in the summer, it's common to see a knobby-kneed fawn following closely behind its mother, and it's also common to see female yearlings—last year's fawns—traveling with their mothers, or small groups of three or four yearling bucks running together in a pack.

It's unusual, however, to see older buck fawns still traveling with their mothers. Eric, who is an avid deer hunter, explains to me that this is because mother deer will chase their male offspring away while they are still pretty young, in order to keep them from trying to breed with their mother or becoming violent toward new siblings.

Poultry, too, live in family units that don't look much like those of their human "chicken tenders." Before first getting chickens a few years ago, I imagined hens hatched their own chicks and raised little nuclear chicken families. The reality was quite different.

A couple of the hens did seem to have strong chick-rearing instincts, and once or twice I got to enjoy the endearing sight of adorable little balls of fluff huddled under a protective wing. But all in all, the hens proved to be highly distractible mothers, prone to letting their babies wander away and into the paws, claws, and jaws of a variety of predators.

Of the eight eggs that hatched, only two chicks made it past the first few weeks of life. They both turned out to be roosters, and after they were a month old they spent most of their time dust-bathing together in front of the house, far away from the only-occasionally watchful eyes of whichever hen had hatched them (I was never sure who Mama was). At night, the flock all dutifully filed into the coop together, the young roos included—but I never saw any evidence of a special bond between them and any of the older chickens. It was as though they'd been absorbed into the overall flock while completely losing a distinct relationship with any one elder.

I'm fascinated by this and other wildlife parenting behavior. After all, we use the same characteristics to judge a "good" animal mother as we do a human one: self-sacrifice, nurturing, tireless care. But in the animal world, there's a big difference: a distinct end to family togetherness. Even the animals we praise most highly for their mothering instincts—hens, bears, elephants—don't sign on for the job forever, or even, typically, for more than a season. And once their offspring have been left to fend for themselves, encouraged to leave the nest, or physically pummeled by their mother enough that they finally move on, in most cases there's little evidence that said offspring stay connected to their parents after their species' allotted bonding time is up.

There's even a phrase, "soiling the nest," widely used by psychologists and parenting experts to describe the undesirable behaviors teenagers often start exhibiting shortly before leaving home to start their independent young-adult lives. This behavior, which might include testing boundaries and limits, acting rude and aloof, pulling away from their parents, or simply disappearing for days at a time, is said to mimic a fledgling bird pooping so much in the nest that its mother eventually pushes it out.

Interestingly, ornithologists say, not all mother birds actually shove their offspring out of the nest; some species instead simply stop feeding their young until the babies leave on their own—an interesting yet harsh approach that is hard for a "Food is love" mother like me to imagine implementing, but perhaps my nests have never been soiled enough to tempt me to try it.

It can be dangerous to anthropomorphize. When we start drawing too many comparisons between the behavior of animal and human groups, we can get ourselves into some intellectual trouble. So it's good to be reminded that the sort of intensive mothering practiced by animals when their young are, well, *very young* does come to an often abrupt and violent close.

The fact is that as a modern human being I am free of the evolutionary need to protect myself from my offspring's hormonal surges or territorial behavior (which isn't to say I don't experience some less dangerous yet highly annoying versions of it). Even at the height of my fertility, there was no need to create new offspring every year to protect my species from extinction, and unlike a mother bird, if I want to let my older children hang around after they've reached biological adulthood, I have space enough to spare in my nest.

Reminding myself of that helps me feel a little better about the fact that I haven't been all that aggressive about shoving my adult kids out of it.

When I look back at the road I walked as a young parent, it is (predictably) littered with statements I once made about things I would "never" do, then later abandoned. For example, near the top of the list of things I swore I'd never do was allowing my kids to live with me past high-school graduation. Barring circumstances like extreme illness, I vowed, they'd be on their own after that—or, at the very least, paying rent and living by my rules.

My stance seemed reasonable at the time for a couple of reasons. First, I'd never actually parented a young adult, so I had no idea what I was talking about. And second, I'd moved out of *my* parents' home at eighteen and never went back. I'd fought through those early challenges on my own, I reasoned, and had come through the other side—a little bruised and battered, but still. It was character-building, I insisted. It helped me grow. My kids, I believed, would have the same experience, and one day they'd thank me for it.

At the time, it didn't occur to me that my kids weren't actually *me* and that they might have both a different experience of living at home and different reasons for wanting, or not wanting, to leave. I also had no way of knowing that the world might dramatically change in the two-plus decades between the time I started having children in the late '90s and the early 2010s, when my kids started reaching adulthood. I didn't foresee the tech revolution, the housing collapse, or the recession, let alone a global pandemic that hit right when my older kids were all reaching vulnerable ages (they were twenty-three, twenty-one, sixteen, fourteen, and eleven when the world shut down).

It's also possible I'm guilty of a fair amount of revisionist history when I recall my own youthful "declaration of independence." Sure, I left home…to move into a college dorm, partly funded by my parents. Securing a vehicle of my own allowed me the independence of moving off-campus my sophomore year, which I was able to do because my parents sold me one for $350—a steal for a ten-year-old Volkswagen even in 1996. As (very) young parents, my then-husband Jon and I certainly benefited from a variety of family help: everything from job and housing leads to hand-me-down cars. We weren't exactly mooches, but we certainly didn't do it all alone.

But I conveniently forgot all the scaffolding I'd been provided while considering the eventual trajectory of my own family. As a mom of little kids, looking forward to what was still an impossibly murky future, I put a lot of stock in the idea that once they reached a certain magical age, my kids would achieve complete independence. It was my job as a mother, I thought, to create the conditions that would support that transition. "I'm raising adults, not children," I'd say, with the absolute confidence enjoyed only by the ignorant.

I wasn't *wrong*, exactly. I still believe that it's in our job description as parents to help our kids learn to be competent and confident. I want each of my children to have the ability to be self-supporting and to have the motivation to create a life for themselves.

It's just that I realize now, in a way I never could before, what a long and circuitous path that journey can take.

If you don't yet have older children, I hope you won't fall into the trap I did of believing that healthy young adulthood can look only a certain way. And if you do have older children, I hope you won't fall into the trap of blaming or second-guessing yourself if your people haven't launched quite as promptly or decisively as you perhaps imagined they would.

I've learned that we can no more expect ourselves to know exactly how to help a young person launch than the young person in question can know exactly how to do it, that we are all trying to figure it out at the same time, including the parents who, even with many years of experience under their belts, are completely new at being the parent to *this* particular child at *this* particular age at *this* particular time.

Either way, whether due to economics, the pandemic, or cultural changes, my kids' entry into adulthood has been a bit... *anticlimactic* compared to the dramatic leap I expected. And my feelings about it have been decidedly mixed. For the most part, I haven't minded watching their more meandering journeys, and yet I'm plagued by an overshadowing feeling that I *should* mind, that by continuing to open my doors to them, I'm harming more than helping.

Honestly, I'm still not sure where the balance should lie or if, in fact, there is such a thing as an absolute "should" when it comes to our kids coming back to the nest. Certainly there doesn't seem to be any accepted societal norm around cohabitating these days; it's not even something we seem to talk openly about except as a cultural joke. Mothers spend a lot of time counting down the days until their kids leave home, but whether we face that day with a mix of sadness or exhilaration or both, it doesn't seem to occur to us that it probably won't be permanent. These days, "empty" nests often more closely resemble a revolving-door situation where the fledgling bird makes multiple returns. And none of us seem to be sure how we're supposed to feel about it. Grateful? Resentful? Embarrassed?

There's a scene in the 2006 movie *Wedding Crashers* in which Will Ferrell, playing a thirtysomething man who enjoys an adolescent lifestyle while still living at home, demands his mother bring him a plate of food. "Ma! The meat loaf!" he bellows, watching cartoons while bedecked in a silk robe, while his mother obeys his every demand.

When that movie came out, I had four children under the age of ten, and I remember thinking that scene was a hilarious sort of cautionary tale. Let young adults stay dependent too long, make their lives too easy, the scene implied, and the next thing you know, you'll be dishing up meat loaf to your grown-ass kid while he plays video games on the sofa.

And of course, I believed I would *never* do that.

But the truth is, I would be embarrassed to admit how my adult children's transition has looked to my 2006 self. First of all, there's the fact that they didn't all immediately fly the nest after high school as I'd assumed they would. Instead, they've cycled in and out of my house for both short and long periods of time, occasionally wearing out their welcome as I've occasionally failed to set solid boundaries or struggled to figure out where those boundaries should be.

Sometimes I've charged rent; other times I have not. Sometimes they've handled all their own household chores; other times I've been overcome with nostalgia and found myself washing and folding their laundry. Meat loaf has been made, anointed with ketchup, and served to able-bodied young men…at least twice.

What has been most surprising to me about these stints of cohabitation is that (with a few notable exceptions; see the boundary-setting and welcoming-wearing-out reference above) they've been mostly positive experiences. I've been surprised not only by how much my older kids seemed to want to stay close to me and, especially, their siblings, but also how well the arrangement has worked for me at different times.

After my divorce (my youngest was eight at the time, my oldest nineteen), my older kids were often the reason I was able to work a bit later or travel; they were available to hold down the fort, whatever that looked like. As a single mom, I needed help with the chauffeuring and childcare, the grocery shopping and yard work. For years our arrangement felt less like parasite and host and more like a symbiotic and mutually beneficial interdependent relationship. Read any number of books set before 1940 or so and you'll see that this sort of multigenerational living was once the norm and a social expectation, not a shameful secret. While it's easy to wax nostalgic about an era when kids left home immediately after high school to start their adult lives, it's actually a relatively new and short-lived invention. Family units working together and living in close proximity is actually a much more time-tested, traditional model.

We have very different expectations for what a transition to self-sufficient adulthood should look like today, but I have often wondered just how long this so-called "norm" can really last in the face of rising housing costs and stagnant wages. It seems to me that the people who have the strongest opinions about when young people "should" leave home are either those who came from a different generation or those whose own kids are still younger than eighteen. The rest of us—those whose kids have stayed home, left and struggled, or some mix of the two—just tend to sheepishly keep our mouths shut about it.

When I find myself getting worked up about cultural trends like this, I find it helpful to look back at history. Because even if you feel like the only one in your circle whose kids haven't flown, if you look at the data, it's clear you're not alone. A 2024 Pew report found that more than 50 percent of young adults ages eighteen to twenty-four still live with a parent, 21 percent in the twenty-five-to twenty-nine-year-old age group. These numbers have been attributed to the economy, the housing market, inflation, and the lasting effects of the pandemic, but it's possible that the trend persists because it's working: 45 percent of the parents polled reported that cohabitating with their adult child has been a positive factor in their relationship, and 29 percent say it's "somewhat" positive.

But again, none of this is new. Looking at census records from the early 1900s, it's clear that adult children living at home was quite common 100 years ago. The percentage of young adults living with their parents was steadily high through the first few decades of the twentieth century, peaking in 1940, with 48 percent of people ages eighteen to twenty-nine living with their parents.

Go back even further and you see similar numbers. According to an article in *Family Therapy Magazine*, "The Independence of Young Adults, in Historical Perspective" by Associate Professor of Sociology at Stanford University Michael J. Rosenfeld, in the seventeenth and eighteenth centuries it was actually illegal for unmarried people to live on their own in certain American colonies. "Colonial leaders called this system of mutual supervision 'family government,'" writes Rosenfeld. "Family government ensured that rules and norms were followed, that drunkenness and revelry were held in check, that young adults were raised according to local standards, and that young people's marriages were made according to custom and community approval."

Hmm…that kind of involvement in an adult kid's life sounds a little like what we modern-day folk might call "helicopter parenting," eh?

And while that level of intensive involvement in a young adult's affairs may have eased up, data show that from 1880 until about 1940, most unmarried young adults—men and women alike—usually lived with their parents or with relatives or other families. The percentage of young unmarried women living with their parents was always higher than 65 percent, with a slightly lower percentage for young men, who had more opportunities for independence. (Interestingly, these days, the gender disparity has been reversed: it's now young women who are more likely to live independently.)

It wasn't until the economic recovery after the Great Depression, the post–WWII baby boom, and the rise of the nuclear family that the American family saw a huge dip in the number of young adults living at home, bottoming out at 29 percent in 1960—a still not insignificant number.

Generational family living arrangements have, throughout centuries and cultures, always fluctuated in response to factors like the economy, family and fertility trends, and community and cultural norms. In other words, it's not that young adults are newly returning or staying home. It's the whole idea of completely independent young-adult living that's new; possibly just a blip—and a very specifically American blip, to boot.

All that said, old ideas—even new ideas that have been around just long enough to seem old—don't always die easily, and parents of older kids are often caught in a difficult tension: we may see that continued cohabitation could be really a positive and supportive choice for our families, but we also see it as a source of some embarrassment or perhaps self-consciousness over whether we are making life too easy for our young adults. We look for cultural justifications for the arrangement (the job market, the housing market, COVID, etc.)—always, of course, protesting that it's only temporary.

The problem with blaming changing circumstances for our chosen lifestyle is that it's much harder to set boundaries and standards of behavior for our young roommates when we keep telling ourselves the arrangement is an unfortunate and temporary crisis forced upon us rather than a mutually beneficial situation we freely chose. And often, we have no examples to look to as models except the stereotypical unemployed twenty-seven-year-old living in the den, playing video games all day in his bathrobe.

The pandemic freed us up a bit to challenge that dynamic, hopefully turning something shameful into a necessity and normalizing it along the way. It worked well for me, and I have a feeling it worked well for a lot of families. Does that mean multigenerational households might once again become the norm? It's hard to say, but I hope the prevalence of mixed-generation pandemic households at least partly soothed the stigma. If more of us openly choose arrangements like those common 100-plus years ago and share what we learn with one another, it could actually make it easier for parents to set expectations—and for young adults to live up to them.

At the moment of this writing, there are no young adults living in my home, and for now, I like it that way…but I know better than to claim there never will be again. The world can be a harsh place, and my nest is roomy enough to share. If and when a young adult makes their way back into my home to stay—whether for a month or a year—I'll know, this time, to proactively hammer out the terms and conditions of the arrangement. Hard-earned experience has taught me that too loose an arrangement, with muddy expectations on either side, leads to tension that is best headed off at the pass.

But I can't say that I hate the idea of my nest remaining a bit more flexible than I once thought it would ideally be. It turns out that families can thrive when living together, and there are a lot of benefits to cohabitation that I didn't think of when I made all those declarations decades ago.

And besides: I might like having a younger person around to make *me* meat loaf one day.

ON PARENTAL PRIDE (AND THOSE OTHER FEELINGS)

When Owen graduated from high school last spring, he was the first of my children to walk in his ceremony with golden cords around his neck, indicating that he'd graduated with honors.

It wasn't particularly surprising to me that my three oldest kids didn't carry that same distinction on graduation day. We're a family of contrarians and go-your-own-way types; my own high-school grades were average at best, and I dropped out of college (on my third attempt and fifth major) to become a freelance writer. Never one to fret too much about what my own kids' school performances might mean for their futures, I tried instead to temper my expectations to the level of their interest and ability.

For Owen, that meant his push toward academic excellence was mostly self-driven. While I can pat myself on the back for providing him with plenty of sharpened pencils, good food, and "Hey, great work on this"–style encouragement, I can't take credit for much else. (I also strongly suspect that none of the DNA I contributed had anything to do with his study skills and organization.)

Each May, my Facebook feed is flooded with photos of beaming kids wearing sweatshirts of their freshly chosen college, holding end-of-year awards they've won through athletic or academic achievements, and, of course, posing in their cap and gown, with or without those braided marks of honor around their necks.

Typically absent from these public displays of pride: the kids who were disappointed in their college application process—or disappointed their parents by never embarking on one in the first place; the kids who plan to work or travel or join the military instead of going to school; the kids who have no plan at all; the kids who won't graduate or will barely graduate; the exhausted parents who've spent the last month dragging the "barely gradu-ated" over the finish line (I've been there and have the rope marks on my hands to prove it).

So, yes, I was—and am!—incredibly proud of Owen. He fought through difficult AP and honors classes, late-night study sessions, mind-numbing assignments, and the exhausting feat of keeping it all mentally organized to graduate with honors. It's worth point-ing out that Owen was rewarded for that effort in numerous ways: scholarships, recognition from peers and teachers, applause from the other adults in his life and society at large.

But there doesn't seem to be nearly the same level of societal reward for kids who choose another path or support for those who struggle to find a path at all. In helping my older boys create their own post-high-school road maps—no easy feat in a world that puts a lot of pressure on young people without offering much practical support or inspiration in return—I've realized how limited our collective imagination can be when it comes to the paths our young people take. There isn't really a cultural language for the sort of pride one feels when a late bloomer finally finds his groove years after high school ends or when kids struggle through enormous, often unseen challenges just to keep their heads above water during the young-adult years.

With my older kids now solidly into adulthood, I can see much more clearly how complicated the process of growing up can really be. For many kids, achievement comes much later, lessons are hard-learned, and obstacles are treacherous. Many young people's stories may include details too private and painful for their parents to share. Sometimes "success" looks like simply staying alive or taking note of much more everyday achievements without a lot of fanfare.

Maybe that's why I felt so weird sharing publicly about Owen's successes with that oft-used phrase "I'm so proud." The topic of parental pride is a tricky one. If we feel proud of one kid for an accomplishment that his sibling doesn't share, are we then *un*proud of the sibling? If we feel proud of a kid for his accomplishments this time, will we feel *un*proud later if he doesn't quite make the mark? If one parent feels proud of a kid who graduated with honors, should another parent feel a little less proud of their kid who simply graduated? What about those invisible accomplishments the world doesn't see? The endless parade of proud-shares simply doesn't tell the whole story.

The truth is, there are parents who aren't feeling particularly proud at this time of year, or any time of year. Some aren't feeling particularly hopeful about their child. And some feel immensely proud of their kid, but for reasons that can't be easily expressed in a pithy post on social media.

Maybe social media is the biggest problem here, come to think of it. When we "broadcast" our kids' successes to our seven hundred closest friends, only a small handful of those people will have an actual relationship with that kid. Instead, they're seeing whatever we choose to promote. We've essentially turned into our children's publicists.

Which can make things even more complicated when, instead of proud, we're feeling defensive, ashamed, or afraid.

When one of my sons was in high school, he did a truly stupid thing. There was no ill intent behind it—it was intended as a private joke, but he foolishly gave a classmate access to his personal social media—and the "joke" went, momentarily, public. In today's no-tolerance environment (which I have some concerns about, but that's a whole 'nother book), it was the sort of offense that could easily have ended in expulsion or worse.

He was incredibly fortunate that he was able to delete the post immediately and that it was only seen by a handful of other people—including, eventually, school administrators, who gave him a swift, severe, and yet fair and proportionate consequence. The adults in his life wanted my son to succeed; they knew him and believed his intent, and nobody in the small handful of people who knew about the incident had an ax to grind with him...so it never became common knowledge.

We were lucky. Not just my son—*all* of us. I tried to get that message across in my exasperation. Did he know how foolish it was to joke about something like that and to make himself vulnerable to another kid—one he didn't trust or like—just to get a laugh? Did he realize what might have happened if more kids had seen the post? If,

God forbid, a particularly gossip-minded parent had seen it, or if it had been leaked to one of the endless numbers of Facebook groups for "concerned" parents who are frequently *very concerned* about much less titillating things? It would have been a virtual bloodbath, I told him soberly, with him and our family at the center.

No, he didn't think about that, he insisted, his shame and remorse interspersed with indignation, of course he didn't. He was a teenager, the same age I was when my friends and I brought photos from a drinking party to school and then were shocked—*shocked, I tell you!*—when they were discovered. The same age when I was convinced my dad had no idea when I loudly sneaked out the front door at night and that my parents couldn't tell when I altered a D- into a very unconvincing B+ on my typewritten report card with a ballpoint pen. Teens' still-under-construction critical-thinking and impulse-control skills don't always fire up easily, or at the correct moment, a fact we seem to have completely forgotten in an age that doesn't give them a whole lot of wiggle room to make mistakes. No wonder they're so anxious.

In the days after the incident, I realized, with no small amount of regret, how much of my personal reaction was tied up in what I call the "But what will the neighbors think?" mentality of parenting teenagers.

On *The Mom Hour* I've long asserted that when a parenting decision is made based on what other people might think, it's typically the wrong one. I know this because there's no other weakness I struggle with more. There's a nagging little voice in the back of my head that insists that other people believe I'm not qualified as a mother, that I can't manage my family. That voice also insists that their opinion matters...possibly more than mine.

That voice is amplified, of course, by the fact that, via social media, our "neighbors" now include thousands of people we barely know and may never actually encounter in our real lives. There aren't just my literal neighbors to worry about, but thousands of people who "know" my kids (mostly through whatever I choose to post about them, or not) and who may also have an opinion about how they're turning out.

And there's something about the teenage and young-adult years that can make us feel particularly helpless in the face of those outside opinions. Maybe that's because the bigger our children get, the less we are able to put a protective layer between them…and the way the world *sees* them.

When kids are really little, public opinion mostly filters through their parents. If a two-year-old throws a kicking-and-screaming fit in the middle of Target, the blame (or maybe, if the rest of the shoppers are particularly generous, credit) for how the situation is handled mostly goes to the parents. Nobody really faults a toddler for toddlering, and while those moments can make the parent of said toddler feel intensely uncomfortable, embarrassed, and vulnerable, years later it's not likely that now-grown toddler will be remembered for their tantrums.

When our kids were younger, we had a lot of opportunities to shield our more vulnerable parenting moments from public view. We could choose to go out at times when we knew our children were less likely to exhibit more challenging behaviors, or we could carefully construct an irreproachable public-facing parenting style (never mind that it was so exhausting we'd fall apart once we got home). We could even choose never to expose our real families to criticism at all, instead filtering the public's perception of our home life through a carefully curated social media presence.

But no matter which route we chose when they were small—ranging from letting them be exactly themselves around others and absorbing any fallout ourselves to concocting a filtered reality for others to consume—we, to a large degree, *controlled the messaging*. We were, in essence, our children's publicists, which—due to how entangled small kids are with their parents—meant we were our *own* publicists, too.

Once our kids start getting out in the world, though, our ability to control their messaging slowly starts to disintegrate. More and more people—teachers and coaches and librarians, field-trip chaperones and after-school program coordinators—start to know our children as persons separate from us, and we (hopefully) aren't always around to do damage control. Increasingly, our children also start to see themselves as persons separate from their parents and families, people with their own public presences and reputations.

We still feel pride in them when they do wonderful things, of course, and we are still vulnerable to shame and embarrassment when they do something awful. But our ability to control either potentiality is greatly diminished by the time they're sixteen and practically nonexistent by the time they've turned eighteen.

Not that we still don't try. I know mothers who seem to have made full-time jobs out of playing social media publicists for their grown or nearly grown children, and I'm not just talking about the occasional boast: they're taking to TikTok to get involved in their child's social disputes and to Facebook to complain when they feel the world is treating their offspring unfairly. It's hard to watch sometimes, particularly when I know the kid in question is not as blameless and saintly as the mother in question is trying to present them to be.

And yet, while I see how misguided those attempts are, I can also empathize with the motherly place they're coming from. We all want to feel like we've done a good job with our kids. We all want the world to view our children as worthy. We all want the world to see our kids—really *see* them, not just their accomplishments—and yet, their accomplishments can seem to be the easiest shorthand for their worthiness.

Unfortunately, our kids do not always present to the world as the delightful human beings we believe we've raised. At some point, we have to resign from the job as their publicists and focus on reestablishing ourselves as separate humans who are responsible for neither their successes nor their failures.

And the biggest favor we can do for ourselves—and our growing children—is to learn to stop associating either their successes or their failures with our own self-value.

For someone who's made a career of writing and talking about motherhood, I don't post about my kids very much, at least not in a personal and specific way, on social media. I think that's because I've realized what a trap it can be to try to represent your children to thousands of people who don't actually know them or have a real relationship with them. When we turn our kids into content, it's almost impossible not to subtly start shifting the messaging, to show the sides of our children in the way we want them to be perceived.

Parental pride and parental shame are opposite sides of the same coin. The extent to which we feel a sense of personal accomplishment when our teenagers and young adults do something worthy of celebration can be the same extent to which we could potentially feel shame when they do something awful. Both stem from a personal investment in our kids' behavior and inherent qualities, and I think that's a good thing.

But we can so easily cross over into being personally invested in our kids' *image*, and that, I think, is where things start to get dicey. We are not what people think about our children. In fact, *our actual children* aren't even what people think about them! They're still developing human beings who are allowed to change and grow and be something completely different from whatever image the public has decided to make them into.

We can feel joy when a child does great things, or disappointment when they let us down, without taking too much credit for the former or harboring too much shame for the latter.

We can feel pride in a child who's soaring high right now without turning them into the forward-facing proof of our successes as parents.

We can love a child who's messing up—see their value and worth and potential—without becoming their public-facing damage-control spin agency.

But first we have to see ourselves as distinct human beings, responsible neither for their behavior nor the way it's perceived by the outside world. The only way out of this tangle is to create a distinction between their choices and their worth as humans, and a boundary between them and us.

I'm learning that once the fraught, tension-filled period of high school is behind us, things start to even out. Some of the kids who wrapped up high school "on top" will stay there throughout life, but many will struggle in college or life beyond. Others will simply settle into a sort of comfortable ordinariness. Some of the kids who are too busy fighting through obstacles in high school to show much promise will go on later to do extraordinary things. Others will struggle throughout life. Some kids neither intensely struggle nor noticeably succeed in high school. They, also, can go in any number of directions after graduation. *None* of these young people's futures are set at the tender age of eighteen. *All* of us parents will continue to struggle with alternating feelings of pride, shame, disappointment, and relief as they ride the waves.

More and more I've had to learn to accept that, just as my kids' failures are not my fault, their successes are also not my prize. The only thing I can do is love each of them for who they are and hope they do the same for me, recognizing that to disappoint one another is just part of the natural state of being human.

I'm not my kids' publicist; I'm their parent. Only they can decide what version of themselves they want the world to see. The failures, the successes, the ordinary accomplishments, and the extraordinary moments are all part of the people they're becoming.

And yes, for that—the fact that they are real human beings, learning to live well in this complex and challenging world—I am incredibly, overwhelmingly proud, honors cords or no.

5 SURPRISING THINGS EVERY PARENT CAN FEEL PROUD ABOUT

When it comes to accomplishments that deserve to spark parental pride, our culture doesn't leave a lot of room to think outside the box. Yet there is so much more to a human being's growth than their GPA or athletic record, so many things we could choose to feel proud about—even if we never feel tempted to post about it on social media. Here are a few to consider:

1. When they struggle through a class they hate.

Did they get the grade you were hoping for? Maybe not. Did they *get a grade*? Probably. Take your W's where you can.

2. When they grow out of an annoying stage.

From picking on younger siblings to refusing to shower regularly to arguing for no reason, all kids go through some trying stages. Luckily, by the time they finish high school, most of them have grown out of at least one of them. Gold stars for everyone!

3. When they learn a lesson.

Some kids only have to make a mistake once and they never do it again. Isn't that adorable? Other kids, some of whom I dearly love, have to make the same mistake many, many times before the lesson sinks in. Even so, we can be proud to know that every time they screw up, they're getting that much closer to the last time they make that particular mistake. Pop the champagne!

4. When they do something that makes them uncomfortable.

And it doesn't have to be something big, like trying out for the lead in the play or running for class president, either. Whenever I've felt annoyed with one of my kids, I've tried to remind myself that basically everything about being a preteen, teen, and young adult is in some way awkward and uncomfortable. Everything is changing, all the time. When we shift our perspective to recognize that truth about being a young person, it's easy to see that they are actually doing hard things all the time. Blue ribbons and confetti!

5. **When *we* keep showing up, day after day.**

    Let's not leave ourselves out of this proud parade, fellow parents. Navigating all of these changes, mistakes, lessons, struggles, and annoying moments of this stage requires stamina, grit, empathy, and self-sacrifice. It's hard, hard work—and here we are, showing up and getting it done. Golden honor cords all around.

REGRETS, I HAVE (QUITE) A FEW

Wish you'd done some things differently when your kids were small? You're in good company. Parenting and regret seem to go hand in hand.

Not, I know, that you'd want to admit any of the ways you bungled the job, especially in public. Is there anything less socially acceptable these days than to acknowledge having messed up? We're living in the YOLO, "no regrets" era, in which admitting we wish we'd done something differently seems to fly in the face of "living your truth." Regret can seem weak, indecisive…even un-American.

But regret can be a useful emotion, argues Daniel H. Pink in his book *The Power of Regret: How Looking Backward Moves Us Forward* (Random House, 2022).

"[Regret] is so fundamental to our development and so critical to proper functioning that, in adults, its absence can signal a grave problem," writes Pink, further detailing several neurological conditions that suppress or block the signals that lead to regret. "The inability to feel regret—in some sense, the apotheosis of what the 'no regrets' philosophy encourages—wasn't an advantage. It was a sign of brain damage," he explains. "In short, people without regrets aren't paragons of psychological health. They are often people who are seriously ill."

Pink cites one particularly relevant example from Janet Landman, a former University of Michigan professor: "One day, a child loses her third tooth. Before going to sleep, she puts the tooth under her pillow. When she awakens the next morning, she discovers that the Tooth Fairy has forgotten to replace the tooth with a prize. The child is *disappointed*. But it's the child's parents who *regret* the lapse."

(It's as though Janet Landman were peeking in my windows during the five-year period in which teeth were being lost so rapidly and regularly in my home that I set up a Tooth Fairy Cup in the dining room in order to facilitate the process and lessen the possibility that the Tooth Fairy would be caught waking up a younger sibling or—during a period of particular confusion—reaching under the wrong child's pillow.)

But I appreciate the distinction, here, between the emotions of the person who experiences the wrong and those of the person who commits the wrong. There are things I feel regret for, years after they happened (or, just as often, *didn't* happen), that I have no idea if my kids cared about at all at the time or would remember now even if they did.

In Mary Louise Kelly's Book *It. Goes. So. Fast. The Year of No Do-Overs*, she writes, "What I think will give future-octogenarian me pause is not the big decisions but the accretion of all the many, many small ones, none of them seemingly significant in the moment. All those weekday soccer games when I showed up late, or failed to make it altogether. The playdates I skipped, the pool parties that I missed. The school pickups, the chance to hear all the chatter from the backseat. The mornings baking cookies, when it was the nanny in the kitchen instead of me."

Kelly goes on to suggest that perhaps she is the only one who actually regrets these omissions: "The boys were happy so long as there were warm cookies…whatever sins we commit as parents, and I've committed plenty, surely they can't be that bad if our children can't even remember them."

It's a comforting thought, but I'm not sure I buy it.

Which isn't to say outsourcing cookie baking with your kids or skipping a playdate is an unpardonable crime: if that were the case, I'd have done the bulk of my mothering from a prison cell. It's more that we simply can't know the actual impact these things have on our kids. They themselves may not be able to connect the dots between action and impact. And it's normal to feel regret for the times we didn't live up to our ideals, even if it doesn't seem anyone else cared too much.

That's not to beat myself, or Kelly, or any other mother up. I don't even necessarily think guilt should always accompany regret. But I do believe that an honest reckoning with regret requires us to acknowledge our mistakes. I have to face the fact that my impact, as a parent, has been one of the most important and life-shaping influences my kids have experienced, or ever will experience, and that my flubs and failures mattered and matter.

If I'm not honest about that, I'm not honest about much.

Why bother with regret now, when it's too late to change anything? It seems to me this is the natural time to take stock of the job we've done so far. When we're in the arms-full stage, we're often too busy and overwhelmed to spend much time reflecting on our choices. But later, when we're outside of that stage with all its immediacy, emotion, and intensity, it's easy to see the opportunities missed and squandered: the things we said or did that now make us cringe...or cry.

In *The Power of Regret*, Pink categorizes regrets by four basic types: foundation regrets, boldness regrets (missed opportunities), moral regrets, and connection regrets. While it's a useful framework, when it comes to my own regrets as a mom, I'm usually able to break it down into two even more basic categories: the things I did, and the things I didn't do.

Just for starters:

Things I Regret Doing

→ The times I said something harsh under duress and wish I'd said something else—like the Halloween when Owen darted between cars into the street, and I lost my ever-loving mind in front of an entire neighborhood of miniature ninjas and princesses.

→ The times I blamed one of my kids for something that, in retrospect, was clearly caused by another kid. It took me years to recognize that Isaac's sweet, innocent face in the throes of ratting out his older brother did not tell the full story of how he'd almost always instigated the same conflict he was now tattling about.

→ The times I let embarrassment or public pressure lead to a harsher response than I actually felt was appropriate (see also: the times I said something I wish I hadn't).

Things I Regret Not Doing

→ The (many) nights I skipped or skimped on a proper tuck-in at night because I was too tired. Putting myself in that exhausted mother's shoes, I have nothing but empathy. But if I had to do it all over again, knowing what I missed out on? Well, you can do the math.

→ The times my children attempted to get my attention and instead got the backside of a screen and/or a distracted "Mmmm-hmmmm?" My desire to *seem* like I'm always available, combined with my complete inability to attend to the real world when I'm looking at a screen, is a running joke in my house. Fortunately, at least my kids seem to have a sense of humor about it.

→ The opportunities I missed to discuss big, hard topics with my kids because I didn't feel prepared or qualified (from sex to death to religion, I've had both my A+, "Wow, Mom really nailed this conversation!" moments and my "Was she even awake?" moments).

I could go on, and on, and on, but again, admitting and exploring our regrets—even if just to ourselves—isn't about self-flagellation. Actually, it's an opportunity to put things in perspective and extend ourselves some compassion and grace. As I look over my list above, while I know there were times I could have done better, there were just as many when I was doing the absolute best I could.

When I consider each did/didn't-do individually, a specific example or two may come to mind, and sometimes that example is accompanied by a hot flush of shame or guilt. But when I sit with that feeling a little longer, a more complete picture forms itself in my mind. Yes, I was often distracted by the work on my screen…but I was also under a lot of pressure to earn a living from it, alongside the busyness and needs of raising a large family. Yes, I was occasionally harsher with my kids than I meant to be, but those standout incidents typically happened when I was overwhelmed and they were testing my limits.

It's not about making excuses: I'm not on trial here, so no defense is needed. It's about being honest with myself about the times when things went wrong or just less right than they could have, so that I can learn from those experiences—valuable, still, at this stage, even though I'll probably never again experience the pressures of trying to run a household full of kids under twelve while managing its economy.

At some point, all parents must face the fact that a do-over is no longer possible. The distance between the parents we wish we were and the parents we actually were becomes fixed at some point; we are no longer in the stage of parenting where we can actively fix it. Examining our regrets gives us the opportunity to forgive ourselves for the things we did, or didn't do, even as our chances to change anything get farther and farther in the rear-view mirror.

Owning our regrets honestly primes us to lend more grace to the younger generation of parents, including the mothers and fathers of our grandchildren or future grandchildren, our grand-nieces and grandnephews, and other grand-adjacent-children who will one day be part of our lives.

It helps us do better with our kids *today*, however far in the past our regrets lie. No, we can't go back in time and fix a specific moment with the once-five-year-old who's now twenty-five. But hopefully we still have a relationship with that child, and whatever age they are now, today's relationship is worth strengthening no matter how much water is under the bridge.

And it helps us make amends. Apologizing to our kids isn't easy. It seems countercultural these days to admit when we've done something wrong to begin with, and many of us grew up with a generation of parents who never said, "I'm sorry." Yet I have found a well-placed, sincere apology to be one of the most powerful tools in my parenting toolbox. It teaches our kids not only that their feelings matter, but also that we are human and imperfect. It opens up space to repair old wounds and start again.

In most cases, I don't think making amends needs to look like expressing nonstop remorse or groveling. Actually, that approach could seriously backfire. No teenager wants to sit through an hour-long session of their parent unloading a long laundry list of "wish I hads," many of which they've probably forgotten by now or may not have been impacted by as strongly as we feared. Unloading just to make ourselves feel better may be tempting, but it's also possibly more self-serving than helpful. Of course there are always exceptions, and you probably know if a bigger apology is warranted.

Most of the time, I've found it works to simply acknowledge every now and then, when the moment presents itself, that I recognize there are moments when I could have done things better. For example, I said to one of my sons not too long ago, "That year or so after Dad and I divorced was a really chaotic time for us, wasn't it? I wish I'd been more present for you then, and I'm sorry I wasn't." I gave him a beat to respond—which he did graciously but briefly—and then we moved on.

An opportunity to make amends doesn't have to turn into a tearful confession to leave an impact, and I believe that sincere and simple acknowledgment of regret on my part was a small but significant building block in my overall relationship with my adult son. An apology applied sincerely, simply, unselfishly, and sparingly can go a long way.

Also, let's remember this: we *still have time*. Parenting doesn't end when your child moves out, and we still have opportunities to guide, lead, and build bridges. What you're doing today, whether your child is ten or fifteen or twenty-seven, still matters.

I think it's also worth pointing out that not all our regrets about parenting necessarily revolve around the ways we did or didn't parent. It's very possible you also have regrets about times you let yourself down, too. We tend to hear truisms over and over about how we'll never regret time we spent with our children, but that isn't necessarily universally true. Perhaps you sacrificed an opportunity that you now wish you hadn't passed up.

In *It. Goes. So. Fast.* Kelly acknowledges this seemingly counter-intuitive dilemma. "I have rarely regretted the times when work and family collided and I chose family. But rarely is not never, and there are moments that haunt me," she writes. As a journalist, Kelly likely passed up opportunities that were truly once-in-a-lifetime historic events. Perhaps your personal opportunities missed seem a bit less momentous, but that doesn't make them less important.

So if you feel regretful about times you didn't put yourself—your health, your career, your self-expression—first, rest assured: that feeling doesn't make you selfish. It just makes you a normal parent who, like most, gave and gave and gave and realized late in the game that nobody would be rewarding you for the pieces of yourself you sacrificed along the way. Often, those sacrifices are worth it in the end. But when you realize in midlife that you missed an opportunity you'll likely never have again and you can't identify the actual benefit of having sacrificed that dream, it can be a very bitter pill to swallow. Swallow it anyway. Taking stock of our regrets is an important exercise, albeit a painful one by necessity.

I want to mention one more sort of regret, one that encompasses more than just a single example of neglect, or a momentary lapse of judgment or control. Sometimes our regrets are simply bigger, and more potentially life-altering, than that.

Big, life-changing regrets perhaps fall into their own category. They aren't as singular and specific as wishing you hadn't matched your four-year-old's spectacular public meltdown at the swimming pool; they often involve many decisions encapsulated as one, and the ripple of consequences from this one choice could add up to a life very different from the one you dreamed of leading.

It's also not necessarily the sort of regret where you can point to a specific outcome and say, "This situation would have gone better if we'd done X instead of Y." Those sorts of regrets can be almost comforting in their limited nature: you see the thing you did, or didn't do, and the impact it made; you realize the outcome would have been better if you'd done this other thing instead; you acknowledge that it's too late to change this instance now but file the information away for future reference. You make amends, and you move on.

But when I think back on my parenting "wish-I-had-and-hadn'ts," often a broader regret surfaces: I regret not continuing to homeschool my children beyond a single exploratory year when Jacob was in first grade.

He didn't learn to read as quickly as I'd hoped, and I felt judgment and pressure from family and friends—whether real or imagined, I'm honestly not sure—to enroll him in school. And while his school experiences were mostly positive, there is something about giving up on that lifestyle—one that I think would have been a good fit for my temperament and nonconformist approach to life—that I've never quite gotten over.

To wish we had chosen a completely different sort of lifestyle—as homeschooling my kids would have required—is, in a way, to wish that we had lived a completely different sort of life. It would have changed everything: the kids' friends; the ways we spent our time; my work; even, most likely, the place where we wound up living, since we chose the town where all five of my kids have gone to high school based on the simplicity of living in a small town with a solid public school system instead of nearly limitless choices with a high degree of complication, like we'd faced when we lived in a bigger city.

For years, that wistful longing was front and center in every school decision we made, and even today I feel twinges of regret. "That could be me," I used to think when I enviously encountered a homeschool mom. But it wasn't, and it wasn't, and it wasn't, until enough time passed that it could no longer be.

It's not that our public school experience was terrible (it wasn't), or that I think homeschooling is best for everyone (I do not). It's that I think I would have been good at it, and that my family would have benefited from it, and there's a certain regret in realizing that we missed out on this particular version of our story.

I hold no ill will toward the younger version of myself who let outside voices get in her head. I have endless compassion for that mom, actually. What I regret is that we bailed for reasons I now realize didn't come from my deepest intuition about what my family and I needed. And I wish I'd had the courage, at the time, to choose our own way.

Of course, I can't know if we actually would have liked homeschooling, and it's far too late to do anything about it now. But I still think these bigger, "life not lived" regrets are valuable to examine, because they tell us so much about ourselves. When I look back at my motivation for quitting, I understand more about other choices I've made over time and how I might make different ones in the future.

There's a much bigger regret in feeling like I missed out on a more essential version of myself than in simply acknowledging a onetime mistake. In a way, my decision to bail on homeschooling is symbolic of other times I've thrown in the towel on something I really wanted to do, in favor of doing the thing that was more expected of me, that would please other people in my life, or that society was already set up to support. That's my real regret, it turns out. And there is plenty of learning to be had from recognizing that.

Engaging with our regrets is hard and messy work. There's a good chance you've read this chapter and thought, "No thanks, I'm not in a place where I can do this right now." I've been there, in times when I wasn't ready to address a painful period from my past, particularly one in which I disappointed people or disappointed myself in the way I treated the most important people in my life—namely, my kids. By all means, put a practice of regret on pause until you're ready to grapple with the feelings it's likely to bring up.

But I think you might find that feeling and expressing regret aren't the bogeymen they might seem at first. You might find, instead, that identifying your own regrets is the beginning of a cathartic process that can help you release guilt, treat yourself and others with more compassion, strengthen bonds with your family, and even make more authentic, satisfying choices in the future. It's worth a try—and you can start anytime.

THE NEW RULES OF THE GAME:

DEVELOPING A PARENTING PHILOSOPHY WHEN YOUR KIDS AREN'T SO LITTLE

---

ike many moms, I started off my parenting journey as a bit of an overachiever. But by the time I got pregnant with Will, almost six years after my oldest was born, a series of circumstances had changed our lives drastically to the extent where I no longer had the free time (or, frankly, the budget) to follow every intensive parenting practice I'd once ascribed to.

At some point, I'd cried uncle when it came to trying to look like I had it all together, or convincing myself I could be the most put-together mom, whose diaper bag contained the most imagination-stimulating toys and healthiest snacks at the co-op playgroup. (In fact, by that time I'd stopped bothering to carry a diaper bag at all.) I'd held on to the parenting elements that meant the most to me, ditched the ones I could no longer keep up with—or whose purpose I'd never really understood to begin with—and made peace with the mother I really was.

Over time, I'd evolved into a mother who met my kids' needs but prioritized my own wants, as well. A mother who emphasized my relationship with my children over doing any one thing "perfectly." By then, most of the time I truly trusted my own gut about what was right for my family, taking the needs of both the individuals and the unit into account—instead of listening to self-proclaimed "experts." And I was too busy actually mothering to spend much time stressing about what other people thought anyway.

The result was magical. Once I freed myself from an arbitrary checklist of parenting practices and stopped seeing other people's opinions as the determinant of my worth as a mother, all my decisions became so much easier. My choices no longer had to be perfect or optimal. In some cases and circumstances, they were probably average at best. But that didn't matter. The important thing was that those choices were *mine*, and I thrived in the loose, flexible structure my philosophy provided.

As a result, my relationship with parenting advice also changed. When I learned a new piece of information, I now had a filter to run it through. If what I learned made sense, felt instinctively right, and fit into my overall philosophy, I might take action on it. If not, no stress. I'd just shrug, think *Huh, interesting*, and move on.

At some point, though, I realized that the philosophy that had gotten me through those information-packed baby, toddler, and preschooler years just wasn't enough any longer. The bombardment of information and opinions out there, about everything from how to handle teenage angst to how to maintain healthy yet loving boundaries with my adult children, is nothing new—from the time I started reading parenting books back in 1997, I've been absorbing other people's opinions. But as my kids grew into totally new stages,

I had to recalibrate the filter through which to process those pieces of information and decide whether they were worth listening to or acting on. And just like it did when my kids were little, developing my own philosophy took time, experience, and a certain level of confidence in my *own* opinions.

The bigger-kid stage adds another new angle, too. When a parent has a newborn baby, there's a general sense that the parent is in self-sacrificial mode and will be for the foreseeable future. They're expected to shove over their old life and make space—physical, emotional, and financial—for this tiny infant. The priority is clear: the baby comes first. But things start to shift as our kids get closer to adulthood and we have to start making space for ourselves again, too. Sometimes our needs and priorities seem to be in direct conflict with theirs, just as we're starting to get the distinct message that we're running out of time: time to save for retirement, time to solidify our careers, time to make our own physical and mental health a priority.

The questions we face suddenly seem a little more complex: Should I double down on my career or prioritize more flexible work in order to be more present for my middle or high schooler? How much should I invest in helping my kids pay for college instead of funding my own retirement? Should I invest in therapy or a nutritionist for myself, or should I put the money toward test prep for my college-bound kid? Do I stay up late and sacrifice much-needed sleep to make space for a late-night conversation with my teen? For those whose aging parents need extra care, there's yet another person or people whose needs become part of the equation. Suddenly, it's not so simple as "baby comes first" anymore.

Experts may tell us to pay attention to our own health or

prioritize our investments; we've all heard the airplane oxygen mask analogy a hundred times. But after a decade or more of socially conditioned self-sacrifice, that mentality isn't always easy to put into practice—especially in a sandwich-generation scenario. The truth is that decisions about whose needs to prioritize in any given moment rarely present themselves as singularly dramatic as a life-and-death moment in a depressurizing airplane: it's the small choices we make over and over that add up to a life that reasonably balances our kids' and family's needs with our own over time.

Just like we did in the early days of motherhood, we need a parenting philosophy to help us make judgment calls in the moment, reduce decision fatigue, and provide confidence and certainty. Our challenge, in the adolescent years and beyond, is to apply what we're learning now to what we already knew back then and to create a new philosophy that helps us make the most of the time we've got. Instead of organizing our parenting around rules and a laundry list of "practices," we can instead develop a short list of philosophies to help us make decisions in the moment.

Here are a few that have helped me:

Our kids' (so-called) emergencies are not necessarily ours.

"Mom."

"Mother."

"Mama."

"Help. I'm DYING. Can you bring me food?"

I get messages like this, sent in rapid succession, every so often from Clara during the school day. My response is predictably conflicted. First, I am hit, deep in my gut, with a response akin to panic. *She called me "Mama"! She asked for help! She is hungry and needs food! She says she's DYING!*

Then, my logical side kicks in. She woke up in a house with a fridge and pantry overflowing with food, which she could have grabbed on her way out the door this morning—or perhaps she could have actually come down early enough to eat breakfast as suggested. Lunch is in half an hour. She will not actually die. Also, she is fifteen years old, not an infant.

As I come down from my moment of panic, my feelings of worry are replaced by irritation. Doesn't she know I'm busy during the day? Why does she have to be so dramatic?

Still, I used to spend several minutes texting her back, trying to problem-solve for her. Did she have a snack in her backpack? How about a friend? Would her teacher take pity on her and let her go to lunch early? I have, I'm embarrassed to say, put work deadlines aside, interrupted conversations with my husband or a friend, and even pulled my car over to talk Clara down from her so-called "emergency."

These days, I'm much more likely to say something short and sweet like, "Aw, sorry to hear. Lunch is soon. I love you!" and then go about my day. When I'm in the middle of something, I may not respond at all for an hour or two. By that point, of course, the "crisis" has almost always passed.

My gut-level instinct to protect and care for my children sometimes momentarily overrides logic. It's as though, for a moment, I forget that Clara is nearly an adult who is capable of learning to care for her own hunger needs. My body is instantly primed, ready to jump in and rescue her. I think that response is probably pretty normal, as is the irritation when the logic side of my brain catches up and realizes that the fact I've been duped is on me.

I'm not sure there's much I can do about the way the prehistoric part of my brain initially perceives my kids' problems. But what I'm *not* doing anymore is immediately jumping in to solve an "emergency" like this one, because it's (a) not really an emergency and (b) not mine to solve.

And by not jumping in to fix it—not even trying to talk her down and offer solutions like I once might have—I'm rewiring my brain's response to texts like this. I'm finding that the less emotionally invested my response, the less the issue disrupts my day and the less anxiety and irritation I experience after. The more I act calm and logical, the more calm and logical I feel.

One day I asked Clara if she'd been consistently feeling hungry or tired in school. It occurred to me that there could be some sort of medical issue if her blood sugar was fluctuating a lot.

She looked blankly at me.

"You know, because you message me pretty regularly saying you're starving to death," I pointed out.

"Oh," she said, with a little smile. "I just get bored in third hour."

Friends, our kids' emergency is not necessarily ours. In fact, it's very likely not even a real emergency.

Our long-term needs trump *their* short-term wants.

One of the hardest things I've had to grapple with as a mom of older kids is that sometimes what *they* want and what *I* need are in direct conflict.

Resources like time, money, and energy are finite, and there are certain things I can no longer put off or set aside: going to necessary medical appointments and screenings or funding my retirement savings, for example. But teenagers are fantastic at making their wants *seem* like absolute necessities, and modern-day parents are primed to shell out cash for whatever experiences, education, technology, or goods we believe will enrich them, set them up for success, or simply make them happy.

There's nothing wrong with giving to our kids, of course. But as mine have gotten older, I've found it necessary to be a little more ruthless in how highly I rank their wants in the overall picture and a little more honest with myself about how long I can really afford to put off my needs. Sometimes, as much as I'd like to be an endless font of generosity and fun, the resources simply aren't there unless I steal from my own (retirement, health savings account, sleep, fill in the blank…). Prioritizing my long-term needs over their short-term wants is a no-guilt-allowed decision. And it goes without saying that, of course, the reverse is also true.

Parenting is (still) not a job.

I've long protested our cultural insistence that parenthood is a "job." It may be the hardest work we'll ever do, but in what paid job does the employee handbook change from day to day with no warning? In what career do you work around the clock with no benefits? If this is a job, I'd like my twenty-seven-year performance review and promotion, please.

Instead of thinking of parenting as a job, I find it so much more helpful—and ultimately healthy—to focus on the parent-child *relationship*. Never is this more true than as our kids grow older and the so-called "job description" we thought we were working under changes dramatically. See the "From doing for to doing with" section in Chapter 1.

"Lame-duck parenting" still matters.

A couple years ago I wrote an article for the *Washington Post* in which I coined the term "lame-duck parenting"—my name for the period when your parental control and influence are waning, even as you're technically still in charge. "[My kids] still *like* me—I hope, anyway—but I'm not quite as essential to their sense of selves as I once was," I wrote. "The self-protective urge to pull away at this stage can be strong—after all, they don't seem to need me or want me around, right? And the empty-nest years are so close I can practically touch those tidy bathroom counters. It would be so easy, so effortless, to phone in the rest of my term by retreating to a safe and comfortable place in the past, or jumping ahead to an exciting new future." But, as I went on to write in the article—and as I explore as one of the basic premises of this book—neither is possible. A lot of growth is still happening in the lame-duck period of parenting. Our influence is still real. And we've still got a job to do.

Risk is relative (and necessary).

Now that I'm the mom of older kids, life is full of opportunities to let my offspring make their own decisions, both high-risk and low-stakes. But as a modern parent, I can't always tell the difference. By now most parents of teens have heard the metaphors equating teenagers with toddlers and risky decisions with hot stoves. Back off and give them space to figure things out, we're told—just keep them away from the "hot stoves" of young adulthood.

But what do we do when every decision feels like a hot stove—often, in fact, a blazing inferno?

Ramped-up warnings via news and social media combined with the complete lack of plausible deniability (there's no excuse anymore for being ignorant of literally anything, including our kids' 24/7 location) have created a parenting culture in which everything feels high-risk, except for the things we know actually *are*—including leading a sedentary, screen-addicted lifestyle and, it turns out, not ever learning to gauge risk.

The truth is that human beings need to take risks to flourish, and young people need to learn to gauge risk to keep themselves safe. We do nobody any favors by trying to eliminate risk from our kids' lives. As parents of adolescents and young adults, we need to get better at both gauging relative risk and identifying *true* "hot stoves" instead of thinking everything our kids reach toward will leave permanent burns.

They're still learning—and so are we.

The bridge between childhood and adulthood isn't like some locked door that a person steps through at age eighteen or twenty-one, suddenly equipped with all the knowledge and maturity needed to make good choices. Wisdom, experience, and basic brain functionality all take time to develop. And just as my early-motherhood philosophy took time to develop, so is my later-motherhood philosophy taking some time. After all, it's not like I bumbled through early motherhood for six clueless years, only to stumble across a supply of knowledge and confidence all at once: I was learning, growing, and figuring out what I thought and how I felt at every step along the way. Same with my older kids. We're learning together, and reminding myself of that lets me give us all a lot more space to figure things out as we go.

In some ways, grappling with this new stage of parenting can feel like being sent back to the starting line: we put all that work in early on, only to be a beginner again—not my favorite feeling.

But there's something to be said for coming at something with a learner's mindset…perhaps, even, parenting included. And anyway, even when we're navigating uncharted waters, we aren't *total* noobs. We have plenty of parenting experience under our belts that can inform the way we handle the new challenges and issues that arise and help speed up our adjustment to a new stage of parenting. Maybe we can also use that experience to help us make informed, intuitive decisions about when our kids really need us to step in and when it would do them (and us!) a bigger favor if we gave them space to figure it out and tended to our own needs instead.

BIG KIDS, BIG PROBLEMS, BIG FAT WORRY

Several years ago, one of my children was in a serious crisis, the kind that tears families apart, that often ends in tragedy. The discovery of the crisis was in its own way a crisis, punctuated by an array of minicrises that fell upon us, one after another—during the holidays, of all times.

Looking back now, I can see that I was in a kind of shock, one that allowed me to push forward through one alarming discovery or rough conversation after another. But once the situation had stabilized, I kept waiting for the moment of relief to come, the resolution that would allow me to shed the tears I'd suppressed in order to deal with the immediate emergency, to release the breath I'd been holding and move on with life.

What I found is that relief, and the accompanying healing, happens much more slowly than that.

This particular son is doing amazingly well today. He overcame enormous obstacles and is thriving. But there was no single moment in which I was able to say, "Ah, so glad *that's* over." Instead, his progress has happened in small increments, in tiny wins—many of which he readily shares with us and others that are happening privately in his own heart and mind and that I may never know about. Because it's his path to walk, his decision to make, his choice to share or not share.

Some moms are fundamentally more consistent and ambitious in their worrying than I was as a young mom. They start early and endure. But when it came to anxiety over my children, I was a late bloomer: I didn't really develop my worry muscle until they were older and a couple of them were really struggling.

Up until then, as long as all my kids were under my roof, I felt somehow confident that they'd be safe, cared for, and loved. And even if the day hadn't gone too well, as long as we all woke up together in the morning, I'd have another chance at getting it right.

I now realize that the sense of security I felt having them all under one roof was somewhat misplaced. Plenty of terrible things happen to kids who are just on the other side of the wall from their parents' bedroom, and I'm not just talking about the sort of midnight abductions I learned to fear from TV specials in the '80s.

With smartphones creating an instant, silent connection to the outer world, bullying, stalking, and sexual assault could be happening inside my four walls at any moment. So, too, could addictions of all sorts, deep depression, or suicidal ideation infiltrate the comfortable cocoon of my home without invitation or permission and do their dark and destructive work just feet from where I'm soundly sleeping. I've learned the hard way that I can't always rely on my eyes and ears to know what's happening with my kids, even inside my own home.

But it's a hundred times harder to feel a sense of peace when they're out there in the world. Twenty-seven years of mothering have taught me that we're guaranteed nothing. That our offspring are their own autonomous humans who will make their own choices, no matter how hard we work to set them up for wholeness and health. They've taught me that I can't protect them forever—and that sometimes I have to include *self*-protection in the balance.

There seems to be some debate over the phrase *Bigger kids, bigger problems*. But in my experience, it's not so much that the problems are always bigger: little kids can have big problems, after all, like illness or developmental and behavioral challenges. Why is it, then, that "big-kid problems" also seem like bigger problems in general?

I think there are a few reasons this point of view persists. First of all, we don't have much say in the way bigger kids' problems are handled. Yes, little kids can have big problems too, but at least we parents can maintain the illusion that we are still in control to some degree—we can't always change the outcome, perhaps, but we can at least be part of the process.

And with little kids, we can also control—again, only to a certain degree—the spin. Little-kid problems are often relatively private—or at least they can be, if we choose to keep them locked within our four walls. By contrast, if your sixteen-year-old gets expelled from high school because he's caught with a bag of weed, your nineteen-year-old flunks out of college and loses his athletic scholarship, or your twenty-two-year-old starts posting conspiracy-laden diatribes on social media, someone outside of your family, doctor, and therapist is going to know about it. They likely don't know as much or care as much as you fear they do—but it's a lot more difficult to keep adult-kid behavior swept under the rug.

Older kids' problems also often have a greater sense of permanence, a more measurable impact on their future success. The stakes are, in many real ways, higher: not only are you running out of time to get the issue under control, but the consequences scale with age. Having to repeat seventh-grade algebra doesn't have the same impact as flunking senior calculus. A brush with juvenile court doesn't complicate a person's future the same way as a felony charge. And probably no other four months in your child's life will represent as expensive an experiment as their first semester of college.

No wonder young people are so stressed. Sure, most of them aren't likely to do stints in juvie, let alone become felons, but plenty will have a disappointing freshman year of college: a 2023 study from the Education Data Initiative puts the dropout rate at about 25 percent during the first year. It's stressful for parents, too, to have the "proof of their parenting pudding" out there for everyone to see. When our kids fail—especially when they publicly fail—it's easy to wonder if people will blame our parenting, even as we grapple with the reality that there's not a whole lot we can do to save our kids from themselves.

Maybe that's why these problems can feel so big. We parents care as much as ever, but we have so much less control than we once believed we did—even if, it turns out, that control was always an illusion. And outcomes stop being theoretical, a thing we try to prevent with good parenting and the right resources. We can still influence and impact, but not in the same way. The six-year-old whose angry streak leads to small consequences like visits to the principal's office may become the sixteen-year-old who starts a class-room brawl. Did we screw the pooch, miss the window of opportunity, bungle our job? And what are we supposed to do about it now that timeouts are no longer a big enough solution and our children tower over us by several inches? It seems the problems were already there; it's our shrinking ability to solve them, the growing impact of the consequences, and our children's literal size that have changed.

With my offspring mostly scattered to the wind, I rely on voluntary self-reporting to be assured that they're OK. When they tell me they're doing great, no problems…I try to believe them.

It's one of the coping mechanisms I've developed to deal with the realities of parenting older children. The rhythms of my days have shifted from using hands-on caretaking to caring from a distance, which could look like anything from filling out college financial-aid paperwork for one child to firing off a text reminding another to renew their license plate. Sometimes it also involves dealing, often from a physical or emotional distance, with hard, anxiety-inducing situations.

While I often experience a sort of generalized, free-floating anxiety about my children—there's nothing wrong that I know of, and yet I can't be sure everything is *right*, either—right now one of my kids is giving me the other kind: the gut-clenched, preoccupied, specific kind. I've done all I can—offered help, understanding, resources, refuge, and a gentle kick in the ass in the appropriate combination and doses for the situation—and now there is nothing else I can reasonably do for this adult human. His choices are his.

And one of the most important things to remind myself of is how little he owes me in all of this. My worry is not his problem.

I went through a stage in which I regularly experienced

anxiety-fueled bouts of sleeplessness. Looking back, I realize that what my brain was really doing was taking inventory. All the things I'd done as a mother, both good and bad, all the opportunities I'd taken and those I'd missed…all that data was being scanned and measured and weighed in the balance against the degree to which those same children were coping in the world: sometimes well, sometimes not at all well, and always I was more or less helpless to do anything about it.

It would be easy to turn into a black hole of need with my adult kids: *Reassure me, validate me, tell me over and over, in detail, how well you're doing so I can rest easier and feel better about how well I've done as a mother.*

But that's not their job.

So I make sure to keep my own house in order. I shower and eat and exercise; I garden and read and feed my chickens; I write and putter in the kitchen and pay my bills; I shower attention on the offspring who are receptive to it—including the steadiest, most self-sufficient ones who never seem like they need it.

The most difficult thing I've ever done as a mother is learn how to step back, release my grip, and give my kids room to fly, flounder, or even completely flop. The worry is still there, under the surface, and I suspect it'll never fully go away. But ultimately their struggles aren't mine to solve, and their lives aren't mine to live. And as hard as it can be at times, giving myself the emotional distance required to let them seek a life of their own is what allows me to have a life of *my* own.

WHY WE
MUST SLEEP

H ow does he sleep?"

I was asked this question dozens—perhaps hundreds —of times as a younger mother, by well-meaning relatives, friends, and even complete strangers cooing over the chubby-cheeked infant nestled in a sling on my chest or the bright-eyed toddler in the stroller. People were intensely interested in how well the baby was sleeping, because they understood that it was directly related to how well *I* was sleeping.

At some point, people stopped asking that question. We all assume that eventually children begin to sleep soundly and reliably, and anyway, it would be an awkward thing indeed to ask of someone's eight-year-old: "So, how does she sleep?" But just because our offspring happen to be sleeping well at the moment, I've learned, doesn't necessarily mean *we* are. Maybe people should start asking moms directly, "So, how are you sleeping?" regardless of whether their children are toddlers or teens.

Personally, some of the best sleep I've ever gotten was when my children were past the up-all-night baby stage but still all under my roof. In those days I'd flop into bed at night, spent, often with a little one tucked under one arm or lying haphazardly at the end of the bed. I was always a bit disheveled, often bore the sticky handprints of a small child, and always, always needed more sleep.

When my brood piled in for cuddles at the end of the night, I'd say a silent prayer of thanks that we'd gotten through another sixteen-hour wake cycle, and I'd promise myself that tomorrow, I'd correct whatever had gone less than smoothly. That's typically all the reflecting I had the mental energy left for. Getting them all down for the night was a drawn-out, bleary-eyed affair, but once they were asleep, I'd zonk out in seconds and stay that way until awakened by an alarm clock—or, more often, a midnight visit. Only once in a while would I struggle to sleep, plagued by regrets or anxieties. Usually, I slept like the dead. My exhaustion, paired with my natural optimism, was like a sedative.

Ironically, my sleep quality took a major hit in my late thirties, right around the time my kids all began sleeping through the night and my job as a mother became slightly less physically demanding. I wasn't quite as exhausted when I lay down at night, so it took me longer to settle down. And those few quiet moments in the dark of my bedroom were sometimes all it took for a thought—the sort of thought that takes control of your brain and won't let it rest—to latch on and do its dirty work.

Even when I did manage to fall asleep quickly, there was no guarantee I'd stay that way: when I was no longer awakened by hungry babies or spooked snuggle seekers, my early initiation to the arms-emptying stage of motherhood was marked by self-induced 4 a.m. wake-ups, where I'd lie there for hours staring wide-eyed into the dark, wondering where my children were and what they were doing and with whom, regretting all my mothering mistakes and wondering how much damage those mistakes had wrought.

The darkest places in my mind had a way of revealing themselves to me late at night, and once I got a peek, there was no going back to sleep.

As I've eased into this later stage of life, my sleep has improved immensely. Sure, I occasionally still wake up worrying in the middle of the night, but for the most part, I save anxiety for my waking hours. After living through some extremely worrisome experiences with a couple of my kids, I've learned to compartmentalize anxiety, putting it aside until I have the headspace for it or until there's some action to take. These days, when there's something really specific and troubling to worry about, I worry until I fall asleep and wake up worrying on the other side, with eight hours of unconsciousness in between: chunks of delicious, nourishing sleep, sandwiched between slices of anxiety-swirl bread.

But my sleep didn't magically fix itself just because I grew more comfortable with worry. And anyway, anxiety isn't the only reason midlife women have a terrible track record with sleep. Hormonal shifts, our teenagers' odd and random comings and goings, and simply too much on our plates can all make it difficult to fall asleep, stay asleep, or sleep soundly. And yet, this is also the age where we need sleep more than ever. Lack of sleep is tied not only to low performance, depression, and memory issues in the short-term, but long-term health problems and even premature death. Sleep is important, friends, more important than we always acknowledge.

It's compelling to wear sleeplessness in this stage of parenting as a badge of honor of sorts: *I love my children so much and am so devoted to them that I'm still willing to lose sleep over them even though they aren't physically waking me up anymore.* But I've taken quite the opposite tack over the past several years: I now unapologetically protect my sleep.

To ensure my eight hours, I do all the things. A regular bedtime so early my kids laugh at me. A nighttime routine that includes an aromatherapy bath, a five-step skincare ritual, and restorative yoga. An alarm clock that mimics the sunset. Magnesium supplements and chamomile tea.

All these routines and tools help set the stage for a solid night's sleep, but the real secret to my restored relationship with rest was embracing the absolute conviction that I need it, I deserve it, and that it helps nobody (least of all me, and by extension my kids) if I sacrifice it.

How to sleep at night

We like to laugh about the sleepless nights of motherhood, but sleep deprivation is no joke. A 2022 study published in the *Journal of Mid-Life Health* reported that as many as 47 percent of perimenopausal women suffer from a sleep disorder and that the risks to our health and well-being include depression, anxiety, lowered immunity, and increased risk of developing chronic health conditions like heart disease, diabetes, and stroke. Plus, anyone who's tried to function after several nights of spotty sleep can attest that it just doesn't feel good. We need restorative, healing sleep more than ever in this stage of life: our futures are depending on it. Noted. So… *how do we get it?* I can't solve every sleep problem, but as someone who got a solid handle on my new nightlife in my midforties, here are some things that worked for me:

Bring back bedtime routines.

Remember how carefully we used to protect the time we'd spend helping our babies and toddlers wind down before bed? From bath time to story time, we knew that a predictable, calming order of events before bed meant a better night's sleep for everyone. Well, you may not be doing a nighttime tuck-in session with your teen anymore, but that doesn't mean you should abandon the idea of a bedtime routine entirely: *you* may need it just as much now as *they* did then.

Keep bedtimes and waking times regular.

This is one of those common pieces of sleep advice that can be surprisingly difficult to pull off when you have teenagers in the house! I've gotten pretty comfortable going to bed hours before my kids do, but I know there can be missed opportunities for connection if I'm too strict about my bedtime every night. I try to make myself available for conversation: a heart-to-heart is always worth staying up a little later for, and it's especially appealing if I can do it in my pajamas in a dimly lit room while sipping a cup of herbal tea. But I'm just not up for starting a movie at 10 p.m. anymore, and I've learned to accept the ribbing I get because of it. I have also learned not to look at my texts too close to bedtime, because when my grown-and-flown kids send me messages late at night, my mom reflexes—the ones that helped me respond quickly to midnight hunger cries and quickly prevent small children from running into the road—are not always capable of determining whether said text is urgent enough to necessitate an immediate response or it can wait until morning. Hint: it's almost never urgent, but if I read it right before bed, I'll *feel* like it is, and I'll often wind up engaged in a slow text conversation that I can't see my way out of until midnight.

Get outside every day.

The studies showing a connection between spending time in nature (parks, forests, your own backyard) and quality sleep keep piling up. In particular, exposure to early-morning sunlight—before about 9 a.m.—seems to help the most by helping to regulate our body's internal clock and suppress the sleep-regulating hormone melatonin during the day so it can better do its thing at night. And since movement is also tied to sleep quality, active time outdoors–shoveling, gardening, walking, etc.—can do double duty. So I try to get at least an hour of outdoor time a day—and yes, that includes winter. But before you find your jaw clenched in protest, keep this mom-muscle-memory reality in mind: going outside during inclement weather *by yourself* is nothing like the stressful circus it may once have been. Is it possible your resistance to outdoor time is based on outdated memories (for me, that would be the not-so-delightful recollection of a sweaty wrestle to get a preschooler into boots, mittens, and snowsuit, only to have them complain after four minutes outside)?

The truth is, heading out for a dawn walk on hot days, bundling up on cold days, and even romping in the rain can be a pleasure now that I have my time and hands free. Releasing some negative expectations has given me a whole new appreciation for how fun it can be to get outdoors, year-round.

Avoid alcohol close to bedtime.

I hate to be the bearer of bad news, but that glass of wine (or two) at bedtime probably isn't serving your sleep needs. But no matter how many times I read the articles linking alcohol consumption with poorer sleep quality, it wasn't until I tracked my own data that I got the full picture. By paying attention to the sleep analysis collected by my smartwatch over a few weeks, I was able to quickly see the connection between alcohol consumption and poorer sleep: both more disturbances during the night and less restful sleep overall. For me personally, a single glass of wine before 7 p.m. or so doesn't seem to make much difference; more than that or later than that, and my sleep suffers. And if you're dealing with anxiety-related insomnia, you should know that alcohol intake is directly related to the kind of racing and spiraling thought patterns that love to visit so many of us at 4 a.m.

I'll also add that a growing body of work suggests most women would be best served by completely abstaining or strictly limiting alcohol intake. My goal is always to find manageable and small ways to start moving toward healthier habits, and for me, an early-evening cutoff really helped. If you're the "I'll believe it when I experience it" type like I am, tracking your own sleep for a week or two may help you draw your own conclusions. (I apologize in advance for what you will likely learn.)

Tame nighttime anxiety.

All of the above tips can help create the right environment for sleep, but they may not do the trick if your worries are out of control.

Journaling, breathing exercises, prayer, and meditation are some ways you may be able to disrupt the anxiety cycle; I've had luck setting an alarm for the next day and telling myself I'll worry about the thing that's bothering me then. I also keep my Kindle next to my bed as a sort of sedative. While I'm typically a print-on-paper book lover, there's nothing like rereading an old favorite book in the dark, with my Kindle set to the lowest brightness setting I can still somewhat see, to help me forget my worries and zonk back out.

And a reminder that you don't have to suffer sleeplessness alone. If you are consistently struggling to fall or stay asleep and nothing seems to help, talk to your doctor and/or therapist, and don't stop until you get some real help. This stuff is complicated and often multidimensional: yes, it may seem that your sleep issues are caused by simple worry, but when we start pulling threads, we can see how our bodies react differently to stress at night depending on the shape of our days, our hormone levels, nutrition, and other potential factors. It all fits together, and sleep is important enough to your wellness for you to pay attention to the complete picture. If you're struggling to get your sleep back on track without help, don't stop until you find a care provider who offers real solutions—not platitudes, generalizations, or an endless wait-and-see.

WE'RE NOT DONE YET

Y OU'RE NOT DONE YET, screams the book title, in a bright-red, all-caps font on a stark white jacket. I picked up the book earlier this week, from a display at my local library. *Parenting Young Adults in an Age of Uncertainty*, promises the subtitle.

It's not the kind of title I'd usually pick up. These days, my arms and bedside table tend to be loaded with books on topics like container gardening, bread making, and backyard foraging. Even as a younger parent, I typically shied away from the kind of parenting books that addressed the cultural child-rearing crisis du jour. Typically, I've tended to trust my instincts and unique experiences over the recommendations or theories of a faraway expert who isn't living in my home or community. And besides, I often feel vaguely suspicious of the authenticity of families portrayed in these sorts of books, the way they talk to one another, the unrelatable, first-world problems they often complain about, the way a few group-therapy sessions and a coached conversation or two seem to fix long-established patterns.

But there's something about that title—*YOU'RE NOT DONE YET*—that grabs me.

"Yeah, tell me about it," I mutter as I drop the book into my bag.

Later that afternoon, I field a series of texts from one of my adult sons, off on his own and, in theory, launched. He has questions about navigating the process of getting dental work done. Will they bill him for his copay, or will he need to come up with the funds that day? I answer to the best of my ability, given that I have never been to this particular dentist and know nothing about their office policies. I'm often both flattered and bemused by how much information my kids still expect my brain to hold, as though I were not only a walking search engine but also a repository of the world's wisdom, able to make accurate judgments about how situations may or may not play out, based only on my experience and the scantiest of actual details. I answer to the best of my ability, and he seems reassured by my reply.

I'm not done yet.

The discussion of dental care and insurance reminds me that I need to talk to another of my sons about our family's health insurance policy, which will expire soon. The ability to keep a child on their parents' insurance policy until the age of twenty-six is a relatively new law, and it's no doubt helpful to plenty of young people who could not otherwise afford their own insurance. But opportunity—the things we could do for our kids—has a funny way of leading to obligation—the things we feel we *must* do. Eric and I are both self-employed people who buy our insurance through the Health Insurance Marketplace, meaning we have to reapply and enroll in a new plan every year or when there's any change to our financial situations—whichever happens first—and the complications grow with each person we include. This particular son is gainfully employed and certainly able to fill out the application, choose a plan, and manage the details on his own. Should I leave him off of mine?

I struggle for a moment with this decision. On the one hand, there's a lot of social pressure to do what we can for our beleaguered Gen Z offspring, who, according to gloomy economic analysis in the news, were economically disadvantaged by the mere fact of being born. These days, if there's something I technically *can* do for a child, even a somewhat long-in-the-tooth child, does it make me a "bad parent" if I opt out? What if he doesn't actually secure any insurance, has an accident, and winds up with crushing medical bills that doom his financial future?

Then, discernment—four and a half decades of life experience in the making—pokes its head in the room. I am reminded that at my son's age, I had already made a number of financial mistakes that slowed me down and taught me much-needed lessons but that stopped just short of dooming me. Letting him figure this out for himself is, I tell myself, *good* parenting. I make the call and explain exactly how to apply, what he'll need to know to choose a plan, and that he can call me if he has any questions. In the decision I feel a mix of discomfort and relief.

I'm not done yet.

Thinking about financial ruin reminds me of yet another adult child, for whom mail regularly arrives in a plain white envelope, its sender most likely a collection agency. I've told my son about these letters multiple times, but he's neither forwarded his mail nor, it would seem, taken action to stop the collection process. I pick up the latest of these letters, wondering what the bill is for, whether I should call and remind him again, or forward it to him myself, or maybe even just pay the thing and remove it from his plate. In the end, I add the letter to a small, neat stack I'm holding on to for the next time I see him. His choices are his own, and I have to trust that he'll learn from them and grow wiser in time. I gather my own stack of bills, remembering how long it took me to get in a regular rhythm with basic household accounting, and swallow down my worry.

I'm not done yet.

My three oldest children are, by most definitions, fully flown. And yet their well-being still feels partly like my responsibility, even as they slowly pull away and I slowly wean myself from being the most needed and trusted person in their universe. Even then, there's something about the phrase "not done yet" that I distrust. It implies that one day I *will* be done...done guiding, done parenting, done wondering and worrying and loving.

Even with my household quickly shrinking in size, though, I know better than to brush my hands together and declare myself "done."

Parenting changes, and just as the relationship I have with my kids now is almost unrecognizable compared to the one I had with each of them ten years ago, it will be equally unrecognizable another ten years from today. But that relationship, of course, will still exist.

My own mother died when I was just twenty-two and a brand-new second-time mom: Isaac was five weeks old and Jacob just two days past his second birthday when she became unexpectedly, critically ill. She passed away a little over a week later, leaving four adult children and five grandchildren—and before eleven *more* grandchildren had entered the world, grandchildren she would never meet.

Mom and I had a complicated relationship toward the end of her life and even toward the end of my childhood. She struggled with addiction and depression, and my siblings and I all felt the impacts of that struggle. Yet I can look back now and recognize the myriad ways her values and priorities influenced my siblings and me for the better. If my mother still has such a large, and largely positive, impact on me twenty-five years after her death, can't I also hope that my own kids will forgive my missteps and mistakes and remember their childhoods with fondness?

Most of us, it seems, spend much of our lives trying to make sense of our relationships with our mothers. And now, as my own children grow up, I'm left with the unsettling realization that they will spend the rest of their lives trying to make sense of their relationship with me. How I rise to the occasion matters—not only in how it will help them experience the world, but also in how *I* do, whether it's in being a mother to my kids, a grandmother to future grandchildren, or all the other roles I'll inhabit during my life.

As I prepare to close the page on this chapter of my life and celebrate some of the things I'm very ready to let go of while mourning others I might just as soon have held on to forever, I also recognize how much will stay the same. No matter what, I will always be my kids' mom, and even when they're all well into adulthood, they'll still be my children.

No, I'm not done yet. But, as it turns out, "done" has never really been the goal.

Part 2

WHAT'S AHEAD

The majority of my years as a mother were spent herding multiple little ones around. During those years, I was constantly primed and prepared to ward off danger or discomfort with my own personal arsenal of tools, from the protection of my arms to a bag full of toys and snacks.

These days no such arsenal is needed, but that doesn't mean my burden always feels light. While I was pretty good at shedding the literal baggage of motherhood early on—five kids will make you efficient like that—I held on to plenty of emotional and mental baggage. For example: the compulsive feeling that I need to be prepared to meet anyone's needs, at any time. No toddlers to mother? Well, how about I take on that responsibility for a friend, adult child, or spouse, even though nobody's asking me to? Or the impulse toward self-sacrifice even when it's no longer warranted. Sure, nobody really cares how I spend my daytime hours these days, but shouldn't I still use them more for other people's benefit than my own?

For a while, as my physical and logistical motherhood burdens naturally lightened, it was as though I unconsciously heaped on a bunch of new expectations just to stay grounded under that familiar feeling of weight. And the process of shedding those expectations—along with letting go of the parts of my identity, even resisting the shifts in my identity—has at times been weighty, as well.

In the second half of this book, we'll explore topics like sleep, friendship, hormones, creativity, and our aging faces and bodies, which we may not have had a lot of time to think about in our arms-full stage of life but that will be crucially important to us as we step forward into our hands-free lives.

We'll also spend some time with the motherhood identities we've inhabited: the ones we've embraced, the ones we've tried on for size, and the ones we never got a real chance to explore. Letting those old identities go can be a painful process, but it's also full of promise: it creates space for the people we are becoming.

Let's consider, together, just who those people could be.

ALL THE MOTHERS I'LL NEVER BE

Sometimes I daydream about the mother I never was.

She was the quintessential earth mother, baking bread and harvesting herbs on her homestead. She brought an abundance of children into the world, giving birth peacefully in her living room, wrapping her babies in organic cotton diapers and carrying them strapped to her chest. The children spent their preschool years wild and dirty and mostly naked, and when they were six or seven years old, she began to homeschool them in a relaxed, hands-off way that still somehow led them to an advanced knowledge of classical literature, philosophy, and mathematics, not to mention an array of practical farm skills. She and her children spent the majority of their days gathering eggs, making butter, and felting wool.

Or…

She was a sharp, stylish city dweller, living in a lovingly restored historic two-flat in a walkable neighborhood. Her two small children looked adorable in their tasteful and color-coordinated outfits; their stroller managed to combine the functionality of a Bentley with the classic styling of a vintage pram. While she took the train every day to a high-powered professional job wearing heels and tailored suits, and could often be found at the ticketed fundraisers of nonprofit boards she headed up, she still managed to spend plenty of time pushing her well-dressed tots to music and art classes, the zoo, the park; she could still be found most evenings whipping up healthy and inventive dinners from ingredients picked up at the high-end grocer around the corner.

Or…

She was a suburban Supermom, darting from preschool drop-off to yoga class to coffee with her group of mom friends, then back to pickup without missing a beat. She lived in athleisure wear and was always knee-deep in an organization project in her charmingly normal home yet always happy to drop it all to play a game with her charmingly normal children. Her house was a magnet for all the neighborhood kids, with a basketball hoop and a basket full of snacks (the healthy kind, but not *too* healthy) always at the ready, and she created a warm and welcoming home that her kids were proud to call their own.

Well.

It may not surprise you to learn that my reality never exactly matched up to any of the above. But does anyone's? Social media may fuel the fantasy of all-in, full-on lifestyle purity, but for most of us, the reality is muddier and not nearly as marketable.

But while I've never had anything resembling a high-powered

job, never could quite pull off the all-athleisure-all-the-time look, and my children didn't experience the joy of living among poultry until they were too old to find it much of a joy, of course there are parts of me in each of the mothers I fantasized about, and parts of each of them in me.

I've canned tomatoes and strawberries (grown by someone else, mind you) while Clara perched on my hip in a sling. When Jacob and Isaac were little, we lived in a hip neighborhood in a major city within walking distance of bougie markets and boutique shopping. And our house had an enviable snack basket for years, until my grocery budget could no longer keep up with the granola-bar demands of a houseful of growing boys plus their neighborhood friends and cousins.

After spending time in a variety of cities and suburbs, we eventually wound up living in a small town where my kids could ride their bikes to friends' houses. For years the soundtrack of my existence was the slam of the screen door as kids—my own, my nieces and nephews, neighborhood children—ran in and out. I gave birth at home but sent my kids to public school.

While I borrowed pieces from each of the lives I dreamed about, I never became a fully realized version of any of my fantasy mothers. And sometimes that realization gives me a pang of regret: it's well and truly too late to go back and do it all over, and sometimes I wonder if I missed out on the best parts of each one.

The thing about fantasies, though, is that they tend to leave out inconvenient realities: general factors like interest rates, the housing market, and how much a twenty-four-hour day can reasonably stretch to accommodate work and children and home tasks, for example, and also more individual and possibly even less predictable factors: disability or special needs, or illness, or a spouse's feelings about living in a high-rise or an off-the-grid cabin.

I've never thought of myself as someone who was destined for one specific kind of setting or another. For many years I was equally attracted to large cities and the countryside; I could just as easily see myself happy in one environment as the other. What I longed for was to go all-in: to immerse myself fully in one sort of lifestyle or another, be it homeschooling mom, hen-tending homesteader, or sophisticated, high-achieving city dweller. Did I just lack enough commitment to see an idea, or an ideal, all the way through to its fullest expression?

To be fair to myself, being a mother makes it difficult to achieve that sort of lifestyle purity: there are always other people to consider and concessions to be made, and I found myself going with the flow of convenience and social expectations more often than I'd like to admit. But for all the compromising I did, I also know that many of the choices I made were based on the circumstances that made the most sense in the moment. For the most part, I've been really happy with the way—and the places—in which my family has lived. And I've still got plenty of time left to experience many of the things I haven't yet.

But I don't get to experience those lives not lived *with my kids*, at least not the way I used to dream of. When I feel regret over the mothers I never was, I think what I'm really feeling is a longing for experiences I wish I'd shared with my children and realizing it's too late now to do anything about it. And sometimes it's hard to remember that what I do counts, even when it's not considered through the lens of the impact it would have on my children.

Midlife is full of realizations, and one of those—perhaps the hardest one for a person like me to swallow—is that while there's still time left to do so many things and to be so many different people, there is no longer time to do *everything* and be *everyone*. The reality is that there never actually was time to do everything and be everyone; we were just too young to realize it.

As I made a case for in a previous chapter, grappling with regret can help us make the most of the years we have left.

No, I can't go back and introduce my three-year-old to the wonder of watching a chick peep out from beneath its mother's wing—I no longer have any three-year-olds of my own, after all. And there is some hurt in realizing that loss and the loss of other things that might have been a part of my earlier mothering life if I'd made different choices.

But it's not too late to experience many of those things for myself, for the pure raw joy of them. Perhaps one day I can share those things with another small person in my life. And of course, it's worth taking time to notice and appreciate the things I *did* do with my kids, even those uncelebrated by celebrity influencers: all the magically ordinary strolls to the park in the coolness of a morning in May; dozens of cross-state road trips including stops at every children's museum in the host county; the countless times I kissed chubby toes and declared them "*soooooo* stinky!"

These moments, and so many more, made up the fabric of the mother I actually was—and am.

There are many mothers I'll never be, and I regret letting some of them go more than others. But I still have the opportunity to become the kind of older woman I can't wait to spend time with—a woman who is still and will always be a mother.

The mother I was is still with me, and the mother I'll become waits to be discovered. I can't wait to meet her.

BEYOND THE
COASTAL
GRANDMOTHER

---

blame Diane Keaton.

Or perhaps it's more fair to blame Nancy Meyers, the Hollywood director whose movies like *Baby Boom* and *Father of the Bride* featured drool-worthy kitchens featuring enormous islands and cozy details like baskets of baked goods and gleaming copper pots dangling from the ceiling. In the 2000s, when her movies' leading ladies like Keaton (in *Something's Gotta Give*) and Meryl Streep (*It's Complicated*) began entering middle age, those set kitchens became the epicenter of the "Coastal Grandmother" aesthetic: the casual yet subtly monied lifestyle these movies have conditioned us to desire.

Like many other Gen X women, and even before the phrase *Coastal Grandmother* was coined (in 2022, by…wait for it…a twenty-six-year-old on TikTok), I came of age assuming my future held a Nancy Meyers–style kitchen and Coastal Grandmother aesthetic, if not actual lifestyle. I wasn't sure of the timing: maybe I'd be in my seventies, maybe my sixties, maybe even in my fifties; but the promise of those gleaming high-end appliances and Le Creuset dutch ovens, the smart silver hair and wardrobe of cream-colored cashmere sweaters and linen trousers, felt assured.

Alas, I didn't consider how I'd actually get my hands on the resources to purchase that aesthetic or the fact that—considering I've spent the majority of my adulthood as a self-employed writer and podcaster—it would require either (re)marrying rich, receiving a large inheritance, or writing something that lands as a huge commercial success. So far, none of these scenarios seem all that likely to pan out, and the closer I get to fifty, the faster I feel that marble countertop slipping through my croissant-buttery fingers.

At least I can afford the croissant.

I don't know much, but I know this: we don't do ourselves a service when we compare our lives to movie scripts, in which it is never questioned why Diane Keaton and Steve Martin look like they're at least sixty in *Father of the Bride,* when they were in fact younger than I am now or, more important, how a playwright can afford to live in a stately beachfront home in the Hamptons.

I also didn't give any of that much thought when I was a young mom. Sure, it took everything my now-ex and I could earn back then to pay for a barely big enough house to fit seven people, five kids' worth of diapers and pot roast, and all the financial trappings that I thought we "needed" to be a decent family, but living with a mishmash of hand-me-down and IKEA furniture was normal for our stage of life, and anyway, I was too busy keeping my household running to worry much about its aesthetic. I just assumed that one day our financial ship would come in and I'd magically find myself the beneficiary of a high-end kitchen with large windows overlooking a bay and an entire wardrobe of flowy designer clothing in quality fabrics and tasteful neutrals.

When, post-divorce, I took a huge financial hit that led to my moving my family into a tiny rental and paying cash for a twelve-year-old Subaru at the age of forty-two—just when I'd assumed I'd be beginning to gain financial traction—I was forced to look at my finances in a newly realistic way. Truthfully, I was never really on the fast track to the Coastal Grandmother aesthetic to begin with, but the setback in my forties seemed to be a turning point. In order to make up for lost time, I'd have to double down on my professional efforts and start thinking very differently about my relationship with work. But, I realized, I didn't actually want it badly enough to do that. I loved that Subaru and that teeny house, and the scrappiness and freedom they represented.

Now once again in a two-income household, after having rebuilt some financial security through a few higher-earning years, my family and I have come back up in the world a bit. Still, it's increasingly obvious that a house in the Hamptons is probably not in my cards. The truth is that over and over, in both my life and career, I've chosen creativity, satisfaction, and freedom over the trappings of financial security. I worked for love, I married for love, and in neither case did that love translate to an inordinate amount of riches. And while I wouldn't change a thing about any of it now, I also have to accept that the way I've done things has created limitations that a younger me perhaps did not fully consider.

And I have nothing to complain about. I live in a lovely home, and while I don't love my countertops (a dark and yellowish granite my new husband chose years before I knew him), my kitchen is perfectly serviceable...though a little too small to support a ceiling full of dangling copper pots. More important, it features a view of our backyard, where I can watch wild turkey and deer meander through the yard, see cranes and herons fly overhead, and keep an eye on my chickens...something the movie versions of a Coastal Grandmother mostly don't need to worry about (it's also worth pointing out that the Coastal Grandmothers who are most representative of the aesthetic not only have lots of money, but also *don't actually have grandchildren*).

As for my wardrobe, while I love the flowy, monochromatic shades-of-off-white-on-khaki look sported by Erica Barry, Keaton's playwright character in *Something's Gotta Give*, I've also gotta admit that my skin tone really can't support that much cream, especially in winter (I'm a pale girl; anything in the beige category next to my January skin makes me look like a bowl of oatmeal).

It's not just the Coastal Grandmother aesthetic that seems out of reach at this point, though—it's the actual lifestyle, too. In my late forties, I'm starting to have the same uncomfortable realization I had in my midtwenties, when I realized I probably wasn't ever going to live out my childhood fantasy of working for a large magazine publisher in downtown New York City. I had done exactly nothing in the preceding years that would have led to that outcome, which ought to indicate that I didn't really want it that much—and yet, letting go of the fantasy was jarring and a little sad.

I wouldn't say I'm exactly "sad" about letting go of Coastal Grandmother. It's more that I actually don't know what it is I'm letting go *of*. I'm grappling with the even more unsettling realization that as a younger person I never bothered to give my middle-aged-and-beyond future much thought at all. When I thought about my future at fifty-plus, I pictured a character rather than a fully actualized human being, slipping into the Coastal Grandmother persona like a flowy silk tunic instead of getting to know my future self, ascertaining who I might really want to be, and determining how the life I was leading moment to moment back then might help bring me there.

I don't blame myself too much. Who spends a lot of time thinking about sixty when they're thirty? As younger people we aren't wired to give a ton of thought to our older age or indeed to consider older people much at all. So, when forced to consider that woman back then, I envisioned my future self as a loosely sketched movie archetype rather than a fully formed human. The gorgeous settings, quirky characters with ambiguous income sources, and hijinks and low-stakes dramas in the rom-coms I watched as a younger person acted as a sort of substitute for the substance that comes with knowing oneself.

I still can't believe, sometimes, how close I am to fifty; how soon I will be becoming my alternative to the Coastal Grandmother. My stepson and his wife are the parents of an adorable toddler, and when one of them refers to me as "grandma," I find myself looking around to see if there's a much older person in the room behind me. Being a step-grandmother has acted as a gentle transition: I still get all the delight of forming a close relationship with a small human without the pressure of being the biological parent of either of the baby's parents. Theoretically I could also pretend to myself that I am much younger than my husband, and so not really old enough to be a grandmother. But the truth is, theoretically any one of my kids could have made me a grandma by now. I'm old enough. Am I ready for what's next?

I know midlife women of means who redecorate their entire homes every couple of years—these women are typically not otherwise employed, and with kids out of the house, this is how they keep themselves occupied. There's nothing wrong with remodeling, and I'll never stop drooling over those Nancy Meyers kitchens, but there's something sad to me about redecorating as a stand-in for living. I'm beginning to realize that, giant islands and French cookware notwithstanding, you can't buy your way to a beautiful life. At least, not the sort of beautiful life I want to create.

We reexamine a lot of things in midlife. Sometimes we need to adjust our expectations for financial reasons, our youthful ambitions rightsized after, instead of becoming or marrying, say, an investment banker, we fall in love with a middle-school teacher...or with the idea of *becoming* a middle-school teacher. Just as often, I think, we come to the realization that the movie set we thought we wanted to live in doesn't fit the people we actually are, or are becoming, as we enter middle age.

In my case, financial limitations have helped me get real about what I want, and don't, and that (when I'm in the proper headspace for it) can make me grateful for those limitations. But that mindset requires some emotional work and self-awareness.

There can be a kind of sheepishness, resistance, or resentment when we realize that our means are likely to be less easily abundant than we breezily assumed as young people who never really grasped compound interest. Midlife won't magically cure us from shopping sales racks, living in a teeny house, or driving a twelve-year-old car. We will still have to make trade-offs, both financial and emotional; we will still have to do the hard work of getting to know ourselves, in this moment and the next and the next, to create the kind of life we want to live at fifty, sixty, seventy, and beyond.

I'm beginning to see glimpses of this future life, this future version of myself, in a way I couldn't quite envision a year or two ago. The Coastal Grandma me of the future dresses more or less the same way I do now; no wardrobe changes required. She spends more time outdoors than at the gym, more time in her own kitchen than out to eat. She still chooses creative and emotional freedom over a large paycheck. She has actual grandchildren and is present for them in a way that was hard to pull off when she was balancing motherhood and career as a young mom.

The full picture is still fuzzy, but the bones are forming themselves in the choices I'm already making every day. Even without that Coastal Grandma budget.

LEARNING
TO FEED
MYSELF

've been spending a lot of time in my kitchen lately, doing
things that ten or fifteen years ago might have seemed impossibly ambitious. I've been making my own yogurt and cheese.
I'm working on a sourdough starter. I've dabbled in fancy-sounding
dishes like coq au vin. I'm even making my own tea—as in, pluck-
ing, drying and preparing leaves from a *Camellia sinensis* plant I
bought from a nursery online.

This kind of creative cookery is the fulfillment of a long-
standing domestic dream that took me decades to start properly
dabbling in. Like many other women of my generation, I didn't
arrive in adulthood with much in the way of kitchen skills.

Not that I had *no* role models, mind you. My mother was a
capable home cook who put a frugal and mostly homemade—
she wasn't above using gravy packets or Stove Top stuffing in a

box—meal on the table almost every night when I was a young girl. But Mom didn't linger in the kitchen, nor did she invite me very often into that realm. Her efforts always seemed to be more about practicality than play, and she didn't spend much time showing me the ropes. So while I felt there was something protective and sacred about gathering around a table with the people you hold most dear, my culinary abilities were no match for my lofty ambitions as a young mother.

That said, I count it as a huge blessing that I absorbed Mom's philosophy that cooking is worthwhile and family meals are important. I may not have learned much in the way of actual cooking skills, but I absorbed an attitude and philosophy about managing the feeding of a large family. The rest, I found, can be learned along the way.

In the early days of my first marriage, I clearly remember a grocery budget of $43.50 per week, which I'd carry in an envelope—cash, right down to the two quarters—to Aldi and do my best. I didn't know how to cook; Jacob barely knew how to chew; neither parent knew much about nutrition. We subsisted on boxed foods, turkey sandwiches, and cereal for the better part of a year.

Sometime during my pregnancy with Isaac, I started focusing more on the quality of our food. We'd experienced an uptick in our disposable income and moved near a Whole Foods; this was 1999, and the local- and organic-foods movement was gaining traction. In spirit, I was all in; in actual skill level, I had some work to do. While I longed to develop next-level Little House on the Prairie skills like making bread and churning butter, my crawl toward kitchen competence happened a little at a time.

And with our quickly growing family, that competence had to

do with a lot more than mastering knife skills and learning to sear meat. For me, the skill that required the most sharpening turned out to be kitchen *math*. As our family's size steadily expanded, the amount of food required to keep us all fed was in a constant state of flux.

When Jacob and Isaac were school-age and Will and Owen a toddler and infant, respectively, a single roasted chicken or a two-and-a-half-pound chuck roast plus a couple of sides still easily fed us all. But things, as they say, escalated quickly. Before I knew it, those four little boys were a mix of teen, preteen, and school-age, and with their baby sister entering the mix, our household transformed into a bulk food-digestion system.

During this period, I learned to focus primarily on two simple principles: volume and simplicity. I doubled every recipe, when I followed recipes at all: most of the time I was just cooking the same handful of things over and over, in as large a quantity as I could manage in our small kitchen with our normal-size refrigerator and range.

I'd never bother making one dish of ziti when I could just as easily make two, for example, and even a full-size jar of spaghetti sauce wasn't guaranteed to cover a whole meal when my kids were at their eating peak. Most often in those days I'd do huge "meat-and-two-veg" style meals. My strategy was to source a large amount of meat (*two* chickens, *two* pork loins, or *two* chuck roasts, the largest I could find) and then add a whole lot of roasted vegetables on the side—two baking sheets' worth were common, one loaded with potatoes and the other with carrots, or one with cauliflower and the other with brussels sprouts.

Pulling that many dishes together, all at the same time, requires a delicate juggling act. Looking back now, I don't actually remember how I managed to get it to finish all at once or even how it all fit in the oven…particularly on the days when I also decided to add rolls into the mix. I *do,* however, remember the feeling of gratification in watching my skillfully executed feast disappear from the table and then compiling the remains into a much smaller container to put in the refrigerator to be repurposed into something else the next day.

While visiting us during our peak consumption stage, my then-teenage niece Cecily remarked once, "I've never been in a house as bread-secure as yours." And she was right: those loaves shoved into the bread box, the precarious tower of fruit threatening to topple out of the bowl at any moment yet always available to any hungry offspring seeking snacks, gave me a sense of security.

I couldn't possibly keep up with the whereabouts or emotional state of every child at every moment; there were simply too many of them. But I could feed them, and feed them well. The refrigerator and pantry, the fruit bowl and bread box, represented our family's arsenal against want, a tangible display of my love and care. Abundance and life, measured in whole-wheat loaves and piles of apples and oranges.

And considering the epic levels of caloric expenditure happening inside our four walls all day, every day, that arsenal felt necessary. At the peak of my food-production fecundity, I was preparing meals for two adults, two ravenous teenagers, two even more ravenous tweens, and a quickly growing elementary schooler. And I was cooking at a scale to match: jumbo-size casserole dishes stuffed with ziti, huge stock pots of chili and soup, enormous pork shoulders.

The fact that the food got eaten might seem to indicate that I didn't have any picky eating in my home. Allow me to clear that misconception right up: I absolutely did. But there are things you must let go of if you are to manage dinnertime with five young kids and maybe get a bite to eat yourself, and worrying about *which* of my brood were eating *which* of the foods I'd put on the table was beyond my capacity.

So once I put the food I'd chosen on the table, the actual eating of it was their business. The kids openly bartered at the table: one preferred to load up on meat while another was always scouting for more carrots; one liked the potatoes and brussels sprouts with the crispiest, most caramelized edges and would make favorable trades to get their hands on the "crunchy bits."

And at each meal, at least one kid would take a polite bite or two of the main course and then turn to the bread basket for the rest of their meal. It wasn't the *same* kid filling up on buttered rolls each night, but the presence of bread or other crowd-pleasers, like cut-up fruit, on the table did give each child an escape hatch.

With the ability to eat something filling on a night when the rest of the meal wasn't their favorite, there was no need to call my attention to the fact that the meal, well, *wasn't their favorite*. Which is good, since that's a fact I would very much *not* have wanted to be reminded of after spending over an hour in the kitchen pulling it all together.

Did it seem crazy at the time? Not really. I was too deeply entrenched, too close to the situation to accurately judge the heft of the grocery cart as I powered it through the store. And it had been a gradual increase, too: one loaf of bread each week turning into two, then three; eggs purchased by the dozen, then the dozen-and-a-half carton, then *two* of the dozen-and-a-half cartons. I was like the proverbial frog in the boiling pot of water: I didn't realize how unusual the amount of food I was buying had become, how large my grocery bill, how many bags I was lugging into the house and emptying after each shopping trip. It was just our life.

But my oldest child's senior year—the last year I had five growing kids in the house, full-time, and likely the height of my family's caloric intake—was also the year their father and I separated.

Amid the emotional and logistical chaos that ensued, I found myself leaning ever harder on our dinner plans to create a sense of order. Before that, our meal plans had usually lived inside the notebook that housed my weekly to-do list or simply in my head. But that fall, I bought a magnetic menu board for the front of our fridge and started writing the weekly meal plan along with our parenting-time schedule.

At first, the kids were with me for four days and their dad for three, then we'd switch: he'd get them for four days and me three. It was a confusing schedule, and I figured having a visual would help us all know what to expect from the coming week's calendar. What I *didn't* expect was how much my kids and I would come to depend on the meal plan itself as a guidepost and connection point.

As I look back now, it makes total sense: everything about my kids' world was changing, and the menu, featuring my cheerful scrawl in brightly colored chalk marker, reminded them that not only would they still be fed in the midst of all this parent-induced chaos, but also that, on Friday night, that food would be pot roast and veg.

Its presence slowly helped me get a handle on the new culinary realities of my household, too.

In the early aftermath of the divorce, it wasn't too hard to adjust my menu planning down by one fewer person for the family meals—but the cooking-for-six-today, dinner-for-one-tomorrow realities of an irregular custody schedule threw me for a loop.

For a while I chronically overbought, then would wind up saddled with frustrating amounts of food left over with not enough humans in the house to take it all down. I'd find myself sitting alone at the table for days in a row after my kids had gone to their dad's house, slowly making my way through the remains of a meal I'd made really only for their enjoyment, anyway. (Talk about a depressing way to spend your first year as a divorcée.)

At some point I started sending the kids to their dad's with bags of leftovers. He'd return the favor, sending them home with bags of food, remnants of his favorite snack brands making their way back into my home just as they'd finally disappeared from my shopping list.

But it wasn't just the changing realities of cooking for the kids that shook up my kitchen routines. Unaccustomed to being alone for any length of time, let alone cooking distraction-free, I floundered on those evenings without kids. Cooking for myself felt strange, and eating leftovers solo from the previous night's family meal, as I mentioned before, was lonely and depressing. I went out to eat more than my budget could easily spare or kept myself so busy in the evenings that dinner on my no-kids nights started to feel like an afterthought.

From five kids at home to four, then three, then two, with frequent returns from the young adults and now a new spouse, the demands that my fluctuating household size has placed on my planning skills have yo-yoed wildly over the past eight years. When Eric and I started spending time together—first as friends in the early months of the pandemic and later as a couple—food was, of course, part of the deal. We couldn't go out, so instead, we stayed in and cooked for each other. Three years later we married, and along with my two remaining at-home kids, we created a new rhythm of family life that included meals shared together at our new family table but in a completely different way from the boisterous zoo of ten or fifteen years ago.

Now I see on my horizon a brand-new world in which I have the benefit of all the culinary skills, experience, and enthusiasm I've accumulated over nearly three decades of adulthood and almost as many years of motherhood. With a teenager still in the house, of course, I'm still putting together plenty of kid-pleasing family meals. What I'm no longer doing, however, is spending the majority of my mothering hours in service to the family meals—the filling of the fridge and pantry, the preparation of lunches, the cooking of dinner meals, the overseeing of the table manners, the management of after-dinner chores, the disposal of leftovers.

Most recipes cater to families of four. Ten years ago I had to double or even quadruple most recipes. But these days, with just two or three people in the house depending on the week, I'm cutting my shopping list in half and still planning around leftovers. I've started eyeballing those half-loaves of bread that I used to think were sort of sad, and it never occurs to me now to wonder whether a three-pound chuck roast is big enough. I cook simple dinners, and for the most part everyone handles their own breakfasts, snacks, and lunches—not to mention their own dirty dishes.

It all deescalated so quickly.

Sometimes I look back with nostalgia at the early boardinghouse-matron vibe that was feeding a large, young family. In those days, getting all the kids to assemble and stay in their seats often felt like running a zoo. It was a lot of work, and sometimes it seemed like a ridiculous waste of energy, when they would have been just as happy with chicken nuggets in front of the TV. Plus, there were so many other ways I was doing for them every day, all day.

But as they've gotten older, the ways I can "do for them" have mostly dissipated—or disappeared. Putting food on the table when Clara is with me, or when one of the boys is visiting, is one of the few things I can still offer. Family meals have been my most enduring and successful parenting project actually, not because I'm an amazing cook—trust me, I'm not—but because I keep showing up in the kitchen anyway, realizing that food is one of the remaining things I can give my teenagers that they will still gladly and gratefully accept, and dinner is one of the few opportunities to gather them around and find out what's going on in their worlds.

My life in the grocery store and in the kitchen and around the dining-room table looks very different from the way it did ten years ago, but that nightly meal still feels like a bulwark against the less-humane elements of modern life. Our time and attention over a shared meal are one small thing we can give one another that keeps us human and together in this increasingly robotic and distant world, and somehow, the act of the planning and cooking seems to solidify the process for me.

Families grow and retract, flounder and flourish, and they are always changing. In just a few short years, mine will once again look different from how it does today. And so the time I spend in the kitchen now is increasingly dedicated to my own creative pursuits—just one more way this stage of motherhood is allowing me to expand beyond the limitations I once experienced, finding new ways to nurture, and literally nourish, myself.

We all bring our own strengths and limitations, biases and

deep-down desires to the time we spend in the kitchen with, and around, and for our children. The kinds of food those kitchens produce, and how we feel about it, are influenced by a seemingly endless list of factors: what dinner looked like in our homes growing up (and how we felt about *that*), the number of kids in our family, the distance between their ages, their willingness to eat anything besides chicken nuggets. Whether or not both parents work for pay, and if so, how much they each work, and when, and where. A family's socioeconomic status, the food philosophies within its peer groups, the presence of either fast-food restaurants or farmers' markets in the neighborhood. But one thing is constant: kids everywhere get hungry multiple times each day, and as their parents, we are called upon to feed them.

We've all got our own motherhood food history. And while your story may not include multiple chickens roasting on a typical Tuesday night, what's probably true is that your cooking requirements started out small—a baby or two, not eating much and expecting even less—and at some point ramped way, *way* up. Whether you're still at the pinnacle of your family's calorie-consumption heights or in the contracting phase where they've left home, are starting to leave home, or are just eating away from home more and more of the time, the reality is that for most of us, those dizzying days of cranking out family meal after family meal is a temporary stage.

At some point we all find ourselves on the downward slope of our family's peak calorie consumption. To me this feels like an excellent time to take stock of the importance of the job we've done. Whether we did it primarily with convenience foods or takeout or from-scratch cooking, whether it was us providing those meals or a partner or caregiver, by the time we get to the stage of parenting where one of our kids is ready to graduate from high school, a household has supported the task of keeping that child alive via a fresh infusion of calories and nutrients *tens of thousands of times.*

That's something to celebrate, whether or not we ever mastered meal planning, or whether or not those meals were mostly cooked from scratch, or whether or not we always kept the TV off and screens put away during mealtimes, and whether or not we were sometimes (always?) grumpy about the whole thing. We did it! We got our kids fed. Let's take a moment to acknowledge what a massive undertaking that was, day in and day out, for the 6,209 days between birth and age eighteen.

And then, let's look forward. We've worked so hard to feed our kids, haven't we? But at some point the pre-dinner, and during-dinner, and after-dinner chaos will subside, and then it'll be just us and our kitchens again. Now it's time to take some of the creative, life-giving energy we've poured into nourishing our children and start to focus it on nourishing *ourselves.*

Here are some ideas to consider:

(Re)establish the fundamentals.

Remember standing up at the counter, shoving your child's cold leftover macaroni and cheese into your mouth with your fingers? Sure you do (in fact, it might have last happened yesterday). There's a time and a place for on-the-go, just-get-it-done eating, but there's also a time and place to begin untangling yourself from the survival-first mindset of your arms-full life. Sitting down for meals, even if you're eating them alone; preparing complete meals, even if it's just you eating them; chewing thoroughly; and being sure to eat enough are a handful of the foundational food habits I've been working on relearning and implementing in this stage of life.

It's helpful for me to think about the way I nourished my kids when they were small: regular meals, balanced nutrition, meals at the table, and plenty of time to eat. I wanted them to eat that way because I knew it was good for them. Why wouldn't I give myself that same gift?

Reconsider your "mom muscle memory" beliefs about the kitchen.

Let's face it: trying to pull together meals with kids squabbling in the next room or climbing up the backs of your legs isn't exactly most sane people's definition of "fun" or "creative." But as kids get older, time and space often open up in our lives and create new possibilities in the kitchen. If you think of yourself as someone who "can't cook" or "hates to cook," it's worth asking yourself two questions: Is that really true, and if so, can you change it? Does it *feel* like you can't cook because nobody ever taught you how, or because you never felt like you had space to learn amid all the chaos of trying to juggle a boiling-over pot and nearly burning buns while trying to keep your kids from sticking a hand into the garbage disposal? Maybe what you hated was the feeling of endlessness to all those tasks, the mess that would take all evening to clean up when you'd been ready for sleep since four thirty, the fact that you had to do it at all. Those bone-deep frustrations can pass themselves off for a genuine hatred of—or incompetence at—cooking, especially in the thick of the post-school, pre-dinner witching hour. But you might be surprised at how much enjoyment you can find in nourishing yourself when you remove some of those expectations, quiet the background chaos, take your time…and treat food prep as play.

Start small and add on.

As we emerge from the motherhood stage when the majority of our calories were amassed from cast-off calories like the discarded crusts of PB&J sandwiches, we're probably aware that our personal dietary standards could use some help. If getting started is overwhelming, try thinking in terms of small tweaks rather than a complete overhaul. Sheri, a moderator of my Substack private community, says that once she had more time for herself when her son Ryan entered a double-digit age, she began focusing on "additions" to her meals to give them a nutritional boost. Instead of simply eating yogurt and granola or oatmeal and fruit for breakfast, Sheri adds hemp seeds, honey, walnut, or peanut butter, or she takes the time to slice a tomato and add spinach, salt, and pepper to egg salad. "My overall focus is taking time to experiment and add new little additions to my meals to make them more enjoyable—and to benefit from the added boost of nutrition," she says.

The side benefits of these small tweaks? The more time you spend playing in the kitchen, the more confident you'll feel—and the more confident you feel, the longer you'll stay (and play).

Which leads me to this: You need time, space, and solitude.

When was the last time you were alone—*truly alone*—in the kitchen? If your response to this question is simply a blank stare, it may be time to consider ushering your children (and spouse or partner, if necessary) away from the kitchen for a few hours on a regular basis so you can learn a new skill via YouTube, putter around with a more complicated recipe than you're used to, or simply get reacquainted with your cookware and kitchen tools (who knows what delightful, once-used small appliance you might find gathering dust in that corner cabinet you never peek into?).

My cooking confidence and comfort level grew by leaps and bounds once my kids were old enough that other rooms held more interest than the one I was in, and I started getting more time alone in the kitchen by default. Of course, I lived in an older house at the time, with a kitchen two rooms away from the living room. If your home is open concept, you may have to fight a little harder for the quiet to play and experiment, but it could make all the difference.

Make your kitchen your friend again.

When you're in the arms-full phase of parenting, the kitchen can sometimes feel like a battleground. Now, as we move into the hands-free stage, it's time to reclaim it. Feeding ourselves is no longer something we need to squeeze into the margins of life—it's a gift that's ours for the taking. So what are some ways you could begin to feel as though the kitchen were no longer your enemy but your ally in the crucial role of nourishing and nurturing yourself? It's never too late to make friends with your kitchen, and now's a great time to start.

THE TYRANNY
OF THE HOT
MIDLIFE MOM

A few years ago, on the cusp of middle age, I was starting to feel pretty relaxed about aging.

I was starting to settle into the softer body, crow's-feet, and gray temples that came along with my forties, and it seemed the pressure was finally off.

But by some dark magic, the moment I started feeling like I could look at a photo of a fit woman in her twenties and think *What a lovely young lady* without a hint of envy, the social media overlords got to work. And that's when the Algorithm introduced me to a brand-new archetype: the Hot Midlife Mom.

You've met her too, I'm sure. The Hot Midlife Mom is in her forties, fifties, sixties, or even beyond. She has impeccably styled hair, often in the perfect shade of silver; tasteful makeup and perfect brows; and an impressive muscle tone with nary an ounce of stray flesh on her body.

The most compelling thing about the Hot Midlife Mom's story

is that, many times, she didn't *become* hot until later in life. Often, the Hot Midlife Mom's story includes a period of time, typically when her children were young and needy, when she would have been considered less physically desirable. She was never able to lose the "baby weight," she was generally unstylish, she had lank hair and bad glasses—until she finally decided to let go of the baggage of caregiving and Put Herself First. She joined a CrossFit gym or started Pilates; she began running marathons or dancing competitively. She adhered to the keto diet or went raw vegan.

So her transformation to Hot Midlife Mom began. And, the subtext implies, yours can, too!

Look, I have no problem with a woman of any age prioritizing her health, wellness, or even her looks. I know very well how those things tend to fall by the wayside when we're in the arms-full stage of motherhood. In midlife we typically finally see some time and money open up, just as time is running out to get on top of chronic health issues we may have created through self-neglect. Yes, yes, yes to all the Pilates, all the weight lifting, to all the facials, to all the healthy foods.

It's just that, approaching the half-century mark, I was kind of counting on flying under the radar a little bit as far as expectations around my looks went. I've never really been great at the sort of self-maintenance needed to look conventionally "hot" anyway, and just when I thought I could let go of the feeling like I should be trying harder, here was a whole new class of women proving that hotness can (and, perhaps by extension, should?) be achieved *at any age*!

For a while, I obsessively followed dozens of Hot Midlife Moms on Instagram and fantasized about the results I might experience if I were to shape my self-care and fitness routines around theirs. But instead of taking action, I just got overwhelmed. The whole project began to feel hopeless. Instead of making health gains, I gained a significant amount of (not muscle) weight in a short period of time. My feet and back started to hurt. My clothes stopped fitting. My fixation on the Hot Midlife Mom was backfiring in a very un-hot way.

Finally, in desperation bordering on depression, I unfollowed, en masse: The nutritionists lecturing about carbs and glucose spikes as well as the nutritionists complaining about the nutritionists who lecture about carbs and glucose spikes. The menopause doctors with their constant industry infighting about the upsides or downsides of hormone replacement therapy. The workout queens posting their daily sets and flexing in front of a mirror.

Of course, I still follow lots of midlife moms, many of them who have great hair, enviable muscle tone, or stylish clothes. There's nothing wrong with being hot, in midlife or otherwise, and of course there's nothing wrong with listening to a fitness or nutrition or style expert sharing what they know. But for a while, my feed had turned into something undeniably unhelpful for me, a noisy, overwhelming, unceasing river of opinions and ideas and hot takes I could no longer discern among, of enviable bodies and skin that weren't mine to step into.

Last year I lost about twenty pounds in the most pedestrian way possible: shocked by my weight at my yearly checkup and worried about a few health issues that seemed possibly linked, I started eating a little less, moving a lot more, and checking in with an in-real-life friend to stay motivated. I'm still amazed that this simple "solution" worked when I had so many much more complicated ones at my disposal...and that, in the end, it wasn't coveting another hot midlife mom's body that did it for me but respecting my own enough to take better care of it.

I've sought out more complicated wellness solutions in the past, as well. I've used personalized health screening services and logged my food in a variety of nutrition apps. I've seen a functional medicine practitioner and met with a health coach. I have found value in all those things, and I also understand that a lot of those kinds of professionals often reach their audiences through social media, as do I. I can't fault them for that.

But there was something about the experience of trying to seek self-improvement through an aggregate of social media personalities, their faces and bodies presented in short bursts, on tiny screens, with good lighting, that simply—and demonstrably—didn't work for me. Trying to model my real-life experience after a social media archetype didn't turn me into a Hot Midlife Mom; it just made me a hot mental mess.

A few years after my detour, I've begun to relax into aging again. My temples are grayer, my crow's-feet more defined, and despite more muscle tone, there's a certain slackening that, after seeing even on incredibly fit older women in my yoga classes, I recognize as an unavoidable part of aging. Somehow, the closer I get to fifty, the farther the "hot mom" fantasy starts to fade into the background. My hope is that by the half-century mark, it'll have receded completely. Healthy—mentally and physically—over hot feels like the only way to go into my second century of life.

How to make peace with our aging faces and bodies

From inconsistent style trends (I *cannot* keep up with what's happening in either jeans or eyebrows anymore) to inexplicably slackening thighs, this stage of life can deliver a lot of surprises. Here are some ways I think we can all learn to cope with the changes:

We can keep looking at ourselves.

With all the changes happening as we age—wrinkles, sagging, redistribution of weight, and the like—it's easy to fall into the trap of avoidance: we walk quickly past the mirror, scroll past the photos, filter out the evidence…

Look, I'm not advocating vanity, but on the other hand, it's hard to accept—let alone love—a face and body that have become strangers to us. So my strategy is to keep looking at myself: in the mirror, at the unfiltered photos, even the ones taken at unflattering angles. With time, exposure, and self-compassion, I hope I can feel less startled by the inevitable changes, stay more comfortable in my own company, and see the loveliness that I know will still be there at every stage.

We can focus on how it feels.

I love a good facial, and I religiously follow the sort of seven-step skincare ritual that routinely gets influencers mocked on social media. But when I think about why I go to the effort, it's really not because I think a specific product might make me look twenty-five again. It's more about enjoying sensory pleasure and developing the kind of calming, consistent self-care habits that give my life structure and make me feel good. The same goes for exercise and nutrition: at some point, the motivation *has* to shift from "looking hot and youthful" to "staying active and feeling energetic."

We can create relationships with our bodies and faces.

Instead of making demands of our bodies and faces and criticizing them when they don't perform or look the way we'd like, what if we tried listening to what they're telling us? As we've learned by now from parenthood, beating ourselves up and being vaguely disappointed all the time are both terrible long-term motivators. We need to communicate more compassionately with ourselves.

We can aim for small, sustainable changes.

If, like me, you keep learning the hard way that you're not the exception to the mountains of research indicating that small and steady changes are the ones that stick, don't blame yourself too harshly: perfectionism and all-or-nothing extremes seem to be built into our cultural DNA. From movement and nutrition to skin and hair care, what if we focused on simplicity and consistency rather than the sort of roller-coaster experience that tends to come from overnight lifestyle overhauls?

I JUST
WANT
TO BE ALONE

When was the last time you spent a significant chunk of time alone—really, *truly* alone?

Not just physically, in a space apart from other human beings (though for mothers, that in and of itself is no mean feat), but where the feeling of solitude surpassed physical definition? I mean: when was the last time your schedule and agenda were born of your own thoughts and ideas?

If you're like I was through most of my first twenty-five years of motherhood, the answer is "Umm, it's been a while."

For years—nearly decades—I was surrounded 24/7 by other humans, attending to their wants, needs, and whims. When Clara headed off to kindergarten and I was once again alone for a significant chunk of time during the day, I was convinced that, with so much free time on my hands, I would be an unstoppable force of productivity.

Instead, I took a lot of naps and basically stopped writing altogether.

My "alone time" seriously ramped up a couple of years later when I got a divorce and my ex and I took up a fifty-fifty parenting schedule. Overnight, not only were my days spent alone, but so were half my evenings, nights, and weekends.

No small wonder I worked all the time, went out almost every night, and dived voraciously into the dating pool as a newly single woman: I was so out of practice directing my own hours that, once I found myself suddenly alone for the majority of them, I had no idea what to do with myself. Accustomed to being constantly "on" for my kids and spouse, I transferred my social energy to other people. Instead of learning how to be alone, at first I merely learned how to be *not* alone in a place besides my house.

Years later, I've come a long way in my ability to lean into solitude. In fact, these days I often prefer to be alone—much to the surprise, I'm sure, of friends who could once count on me for an "I'm in!" response to any last-minute text invitation and occasionally to the chagrin of my spouse, who may wish I were a bit more available than I always want to be.

As it turns out, I really enjoy my own company. It reminds me of the many happy hours I spent quietly playing, reading, wandering through the woods, and dreaming up worlds as a little girl...all by myself.

Alone, I could babble stories or make up tunes or simply be quiet. With no one to interrupt—or insert themselves into—my daydreams, I could imagine the world to my own liking. I played alone often, but I don't remember ever being lonely.

At some point, that shifted—as it does, I think, for most dreamy, solitary children. By upper elementary school I'd started prioritizing socializing over having solo time; by middle school I'd absorbed the idea that popularity was the only goal that mattered; in high school I learned to feed on the approval and expectations of others. Adulthood taught me to pour my energy into other people, prioritizing the emotional needs of clients, friends, and coworkers in addition to my children and romantic partners.

It's only been in the past few years that I've begun to tap into that little-girl energy again, the remembrance of being a person who liked my own self enough, who valued my own self's company enough, to happily hang out with her—and *only* her—for hours on end.

My only wish is that I'd remembered how to thrive in solitude a lot sooner.

Can you relate? Maybe early motherhood taught you to be "on" for small, dependent people and you've had a hard time turning that setting back "off" as they've gotten older. Maybe you're facing longer periods of separation from your kids—summer camp, custody schedules, college—and aren't sure how you'll cope. Or maybe, years into motherhood, you're starting to feel stifled by the constant togetherness of family life and desperately seeking solitude. Maybe it's a little of both: you know you need time by yourself but aren't sure how to claim it as a legitimate need or what to do with opportunities when they come your way.

Wherever you are on this spectrum, your experience is normal. Human beings need social connection and bonding, and yet there's such a thing as too much of a good thing. Caring for children can be rewarding and satisfying, and yet…well, see the last sentence. But just because we know we need alone time sometimes doesn't mean we know what to do with it when we've got it.

I've learned a few things that have helped me figure out my own personal balance between happily-solo and so-happy-all-together:

I learned to travel alone.

When I was forty-two and Clara was ten, I took myself on a six-day solo trip…much of it spent camping, hiking, and backpacking in the northern Michigan wilderness.

By this point, you'd have thought I'd be pretty good at being alone. I'd been divorced for over two years by then, and a fifty-fifty parenting-time schedule had forced me to face long blocks of time sans kids. Plus, I'd been traveling solo for work for well over a decade by then (and loving almost every minute of it).

But spending time alone in one's home offers endless potential distractions as well as easy access to local watering holes and other places to be alone in a not-alone kind of way. And there's a big difference between traveling by yourself to a conference where, upon arrival, you'll be surrounded by hundreds or thousands of fellow eventgoers…and traveling by yourself to a place where, upon arrival, you'll be surrounded by, well, just yourself. And bugs and birds. And maybe bears.

My trip created a singular sort of solitude, one I hadn't experienced for as long as I could remember. Navigating challenges like setting up and tearing down my own campsites and facing manageable risk-versus-benefit analyses helped boost my self-confidence, which had taken a huge hit in the aftermath of divorce. Spending days mostly alone in the forest reminded me what it's like to be quiet and surrounded by quiet—a state of being I had not been much acquainted with for decades. The trip was life-changing, and I highly recommend a similar experience to any mothers who can't remember the last time they were alone or who feel anxious even thinking about it.

Does solo travel have to mean a retreat to the woods if that's not your thing? Absolutely not, but I think what made this particular trip so impactful is how thoroughly it removed me from my comfort zone, away from the easy reach of distractions to ease the discomfort of solitude. Travel in any unfamiliar place could have a similar effect, I think, so long as it forces you to fight through the discomfort instead of reaching for easy and reliable crutches.

I got comfortable with FOMO.

One sunny afternoon last August, my phone dinged with a text that made me sit up straight. "Let's have an epic weekend!" my friend Candice, a fellow fortysomething, wrote. She rattled off a list of potential activities for a last-gasp summer weekend itinerary: the beach, dinner out, sailing, and various opportunities for live music.

I didn't recognize most of the other numbers the text had gone to, but as a mega-extrovert and skilled connector—not to mention one of the coolest people I know—Candice always brings together good people. All signs pointed to a fun weekend, should I choose to jump into the mix.

But jump I did not. At different intervals that evening, all day Saturday, and continuing into Sunday, texts piled up: "Meet me in the parking lot at 1:30!" "Almost there!" "I'm at the bar!" accompanied by the occasional GIF. It was clear that, indeed, a weekend of merrymaking was underway.

Only, it was underway without my participation. Because as the weekend kept rolling on and the texts kept rolling in, I kept... just *not going*.

And to my surprise, there was one familiar and specific emotion that, like me, proved to be a weekend-long no-show: FOMO, or "Fear of Missing Out."

Faced with an oncoming weekend, the younger (even just a year or two younger) version of me would have tried to lock down plans as early as possible. I was typically among the first to arrive and the last to leave: a festival, a party, a night out didn't matter; I was in it to win it. Leaving early might mean missing out on the best part of the night, and not showing at all? Inconceivable—even on those days when a quiet evening in with a good book would have served me better.

I know many of us are still operating from a place of gut-level anxiety about "missing out," probably going back to our middle-school years, when we learned that missing a sleepover could lead to complete social annihilation. But in midlife, FOMO has slowly lost its grip on me. I think it's because I've learned to tune in to that quiet inner voice telling me, "That sounds like a great time—but this time, it's not for you." The more I've practiced leaving early, limiting my length of stay, and declining invitations entirely, the more I've realized that there's rarely any real fallout—and when there is, it's often the beginning of a slow progression toward a change that needed to happen anyway. I don't regularly hang out with all the same people I did in my thirties or even my early forties, and in many ways those are changes that needed to happen because my social circles had become too large to manage well in the stage of life I'm in now.

In the end, my weekend went down the way I'd needed it to: quietly, productively, and slowly. And while I knew I would have enjoyed myself if I'd jumped into the festivities, I also didn't actually regret having held back.

I rethought my self-descriptors.

I've long been a personality-test junkie. From the multiple-choice quizzes we used to fill out in *YM* magazine to more sophisticated systems like Myers-Briggs and the Enneagram, I've never been able to resist the appeal of being analyzed. I've taken the Myers-Briggs assessments at least a dozen times and came up ENFP—that "E" stands for "Extroverted"—on every occasion. I took that analysis to heart, but now realize I was missing a large part of the picture.

An extrovert is a person who draws energy from being around other people, and in many ways, that's true for me. But for many years, I simply played the part of an extreme extrovert, saying "yes" to every invitation and finding ways to put myself in the middle of crowds of people at any opportunity, rather than taking the analysis a step further to ask, "Is this serving me?"

When I became familiar with another personality system, the Enneagram, in my thirties, the big picture started to become more clearly revealed. As an Enneagram 2—"The Helper"—I am wired to want to nurture and serve others. And when one is a people pleaser with fuzzy boundaries, public-facing extroversion can become more performative and draining than supportive and nourishing. For decades, I believed on some deep level that people needed me to be charming, cheerful, fun…and basically always available. Solo time on my hands often led to stress—not because I didn't like being alone (I do…I like it very, *very* much), but because it felt, in some inexplicable way, like I was letting someone down. But I never took the time to ask myself whether I was letting *myself* down by being "on" for others whenever I had the chance. I didn't pay close enough attention to how I felt after outings (not just right away—I usually feel pretty great in the immediate afterglow of a successful social outing, but I can feel incredibly drained or sad later that night, or the next day).

There's also the matter of degrees and relativity. When my kids were younger, my life was so full of noise, mess, and need that even the loudest, most crowded bar or party felt like a welcome respite. Sure, the scene might be chaotic, but it wasn't *my* chaos. I wouldn't be expected to clean anything, serve anyone, or pretend to be interested in a long explanation of something I found incredibly boring. I wouldn't, in short, have to take care of anyone.

That's what it *seemed* like, anyway. But in truth, being around groups of people can require a lot of caretaking, especially for those of us who are wired to look for ways to mother others. The more experiences I've had building my solitude muscle, the more I've realized that being around other people isn't always the battery-charging experience I hope for and that I need alone time far more than I ever thought.

The point of this section isn't (only!) to indulge in self-analysis (though I'm happy to do that with anyone, anytime), but to show that sometimes, in the busyness of early motherhood, we can latch on to certain ideas about ourselves that we've picked up in bits and pieces, and it's only when we take the time to go deeper that we can see the full picture. Learning about my Enneagram type and layering it over what I had already learned about myself through Myers-Briggs helped me to know myself more deeply and allowed me to rethink some assumptions I'd made about my motives and needs.

I've realized that the world is made up of two kinds of people: those who are highly skeptical of (or simply "meh" about) personality assessments and those who can't get enough. But even if personality frameworks aren't your thing, I think you'll agree that it's a good idea to know yourself better! For myself, it was only when my kids started getting older and I had enough time to myself to explore these concepts that I learned that not all social engagements are battery-charging for me and that I need more alone time than I'd thought. In other words, *I had to be alone to learn that I needed to be alone.* A definite vote for finding ways to experience solitude regularly, no matter what stage of motherhood you're in now.

In the midst of a "loneliness epidemic," it may seem counterintuitive for me to advise other moms in midlife to be alone *more.* The pandemic did weird things to all of us socially; it now seems much more normal to flake out on plans or to be a no-show at important events. These are not good things. We need people we can count on, which means we need to be people who can be counted on. In the next chapter, we'll explore what a thriving, supportive, and secure social life can look like as we venture into the next stage of motherhood.

But I think it's also important to note that not all of the changes that happened during the pandemic were for the worse—at least not for me, or for fellow recovering indiscriminate social butterflies. Prior to the pandemic, my social life had become bloated and unsustainable. With social media allowing us to expand our networks exponentially, to consider more and more invitations at any given time—and to experience more and more of the related FOMO when we couldn't go or weren't invited—my perspective of what I "should" be participating in socially had become skewed and *in fact was contributing to a deeper sense of loneliness* by preventing me from being able to invest deeply enough into the most important relationships in my life, or, importantly, my relationship with myself.

You can be awfully lonely even if you're never alone, and while the scaling back that happened in March of 2020 was uncomfortable, and even painful at times, it's helped me create a saner and more balanced way of interacting with others. For me, learning to thrive in solitude has been one of the most powerful gifts of the last few years of my life and one that I believe will serve me well as I enter the next stage of motherhood.

HOW TO BE ALONE: FIVE WAYS TO EMBRACE SOLITUDE

If you're accustomed to being busy, tend toward extraversion, or are just out of practice spending time alone (join the club, Mama), it can be daunting—and even uncomfortable—to keep yourself company. (See also: looking forward to a quiet evening alone and then accidentally spending the whole night scrolling mindlessly. Whoops!)

Here are some ways to get more comfortable with alone time if you're out of practice:

1. **Keep a running list of solo activities**
    These don't have to be anything earth-shattering: reading a book in the bathtub, taking a walk with just your own thoughts, or sitting alone in a coffee shop all count. You've been meaning to try so that when the opportunity arises, you've got inspiration. By making a list, when the opportunity arises, you'll have inspiration..

2. **Get out of the house.**
    Some of us love to putter at home; others feel stuck or squirrelly. If you're in the latter category, practice alone time by

taking yourself on a coffee date with a good magazine, or go on a stroll with some music in your headphones.

3. Put it on the calendar.

It's nice to think you'll just naturally take advantage of opportunities for alone time, but that's a good way to wind up five episodes into a Hulu binge or at the "worried about the state of humanity" point of Instagram scrolling. That's not to say that some judicious screen time can't be part of a healthy solitude diet, but there's so much more possibility out there for you to explore! Start by penciling it into your schedule so you'll be sure to take—or make—the time.

4. Practice saying "no"

(or, better yet, saying nothing—at least not right away). A lesson that was hard-learned but life-changing for me: an invitation does not require an immediate response. I am allowed to take my time considering, and I'm equally allowed to say, "No thanks, I'm staying in tonight," even if I have nothing compelling happening at home.

5. Enlist help from a partner or friend.

If getting more time alone is important to you but you keep finding yourself filling time with other people's agendas, try asking someone you trust to check in with you every now and then to hold you accountable.

FRIEND ME
LIKE A BOOMER

———————————

Growing up, I didn't give a lot of thought to my mother's social life—but I know for sure that she had one. We went to church every Sunday, arriving early enough for her adult Bible study and lingering long afterward for coffee hour. She had local friends who'd stop by for a cup of coffee and a chat on the weekend or whose houses we'd go to on weekday evenings. The moms of the kids my mom watched in her in-home daycare were friends of a sort, too; they'd often linger to chat while picking up their little ones after work. And then there were the phone calls: hours-long affairs in which Mom would pace a path between the living room and kitchen, curled cord stretching and tangling one way and then the other, while she caught up with one of her sisters, or her sister-in-law, or her *ex*-sister-in-law, or her best friend from high school, all women who lived too far away to visit often but who remained tethered via this simple ritual.

When I became a mother, it was still the era of the phone call. Smartphones didn't exist yet, and most people I knew didn't yet own a cell phone on which to text. I talked regularly on the phone in those days: with my mother, my high-school friends, my sister. But there was another era dawning, too: the internet era. Hungry for companionship with other mothers, and not sure where to find them as a twenty-year-old recent ex-college student, I went online in search of support. I found that, and a lot of other things, too, as I wandered into the world of ICQ chat, AOL Instant Messenger or AIM, and forums.

It was a different internet world in those days, and a mostly anonymous one: pre-Facebook, people usually used handles instead of their actual names to communicate. And while there was plenty of trolling and mean-spirited commenting in those days, there was a safe, cloistered feeling in those internet-based discussions. With limited means to "broadcast" our ideas to a larger audience, the relationships we created—while still digital in nature—were relatively intimate, in small groups and one-on-one. When you hit it off with a particular person in a forum, you'd often take your conversation to a private message. I remember long, funny, emotional conversations with other mothers in those days, some of whom I now remember only as a username. It might seem impersonal, but those women were a very real and personal lifeline during a time when my life was often lonely and overwhelming—sort of my early 2000s version of my mother's lengthy phone calls.

As we all know, the popularity of those early forums and instant messaging platforms slowly gave way to new ways of communicating, ways that could more easily scale and therefore be more easily monetized. Opinionated forum members began to leave in favor of starting blogs, where they could say whatever they wanted without moderation. Then Facebook centralized and publicized online conversation, the final nail in the coffin to forums as they existed in the early 2000s. As social media grew, blogging started to feel less engaged: why bother leaving a comment when you could just react to what you'd read on your own Instagram account and maybe launch your own minimedia empire at the same time?

Theoretically, social media and smartphones *could* provide the same sort of intimacy that those old-school AIM conversations once did. But I get the feeling most of us aren't using them that way. My own social media usage has devolved into mostly scrolling and consuming snippets of content promoting other people's lives (plus cat videos, of course) with occasional self-promotion, because it's starting to seem like this is what these platforms are really for. Everyone's an influencer. And when you use the same technology to broadcast as you ostensibly do to connect, it's hard not to let one purpose begin to spill over into the other. Am I really "talking to my friends" when I post something to seven thousand people on Instagram?

I was reminded of the difference between friendship in my mother's era and now when I recently spent a week with my seventy-eight-year-old aunt. Struggling with a variety of health issues, she needed help packing up her house, getting it ready for sale, and managing showings, in addition to caring for her small dog.

The visit was remarkable in that it showed me how a widowed woman living alone for twenty years nonetheless had built a vibrant social life that sustained her right until the end. During the day, we'd grab Scottie Pippen, her Cavalier King Charles spaniel, and head to the local dog park where Aunt Paula and especially Scottie were practically celebrities. In the late afternoon, we might meet up with a friend for an early dinner, and we spent hours texting other friends to set up lunch dates (her calendar never had more than a few days between in-person get-togethers on it.) In the evening, settled into her recliner with a glass of Scotch and *Law & Order: SVU* on the TV, she'd begin her usual ritual of calling one of her friends—several of whom she'd known for decades—on the phone and talking for hours.

Sitting in the other room listening, I marveled at these long, chatty conversations, wondering when the last time was that I'd called a friend just to catch up. My phone's recent incoming calls are mostly spam, and my outgoing calls are mostly perfunctory, one- to two-minute affairs, just long enough when my hands are too full to type to nail down fuzzy details or ask my husband to pick me up a specific item at the store.

Sure, my friends and I keep up with one another via text, as most people do these days, and we're pretty good at staying connected, modern lifestyles and teenage kids considered. But listening to my aunt spend hours on the phone every evening created a nostalgic tug to be more connected. It reminded me of being a teenager, lying on the sofa in the little sitting room off the kitchen, with my feet in the air, phone cord stretched as far as it would go, talking to an array of friends about boys and teachers and Homecoming.

These days, we have more advanced technology than a phone line, which can add some interesting possibilities to the way we connect. During the early pandemic, people pushed those possibilities to the limits. I "attended" multiple Zoom birthday parties. In a fit of boredom-fueled creativity, my business partner, Sarah, and a group of her old friends wriggled into their wedding dresses (with varying degrees of zipper engagement) for a Zoom girl's night. Seeing familiar faces on a screen felt like a lifeline during a time when our social worlds had been shattered, but there's a reason, I think, that Zoom exploded for work but didn't quite catch on as a replacement for other forms of socializing. Scheduling an on-screen call with multiple people is a lot more complicated, and a lot less intimate, than simply lifting a receiver, dialing a friend's number, and hoping they answer.

Much has been made of the younger Millennial and Gen Z fear of, or resistance to, using the phone to place calls. I hope these generations have a chance to learn that there is nothing to fear and everything to gain from experiencing long-distance friends one-on-one via the subtleties of their voice: tone, pacing, sighs and exclamations, the intimacy of paying attention to just one person at a time and really *hearing* what they have to say.

But even having a good old nostalgic phone call can't compete with getting together in the flesh. Each summer I go on a getaway weekend with two of the friends I might have been on the phone with: Jenna and Missy, my besties since high school. While we do a decent job staying connected the rest of the year—we all three now live in the same community, and Jenna married my brother, so it's not too hard to stay at least loosely in touch—our getaway is the yearly high point of our three-way friendship. We talk about literally everything, as you can with women you've known for three-plus decades: motherhood, work, marriage, and, increasingly, what's happening with our aging bodies and faces.

On our trip a couple of years ago, as I stood in front of the bathroom mirror blow-drying my hair, I made the discovery that, when the blow-dryer was set to high and pointed in just the right direction at my neck, the high velocity turned that little crease at the front of my neck—if you're over forty, you know the one—into a rippling wave, like the surface of a pond on a windy day.

I shrieked, first with horror and then with hysterical laughter, and my friends came running. They howled as I showed them my discovery, rippling my neck over and over as the three of us laughed, doubled over in turns, until we couldn't breathe and tears streamed from our eyes. I still laugh every time I think about it, and they still laugh every time I remind them.

When I think about that moment, I'm struck, too, by the singular experience of sharing a moment like that with close friends. I absolutely would not have been able to have the same experience with my loving husband, who may have been amused but who probably would have swallowed any possibility of a laugh for fear of hurting my feelings. I also suspect that posting a video of my rippling-neck trick on social media would have fallen flat: to a stranger, absent context, it would have been more cringe-inducing than funny to watch. No, the moment was so gut-achingly funny in that specific circumstance due to a combination of *intimacy* and *shared experience.*

Eric and I enjoy plenty of intimacy, but not a shared experience of midlife womanhood. Fortysomething acquaintances on the internet may share my experience of midlife womanhood, but not the intimacy with me to find my particular moment so hilarious. But Jenna and Missy and I know one another well enough, and are close enough, that we've shared in many of life's most significant—and awkward—moments already: embarrassing teenage crushes and college parties gone awry; weddings, pregnancies, births; divorces and near divorces; and lately, increasingly visible signs of aging. My gently rippling pond of a neck was just one more such sign to throw on the pile of indignities we'd all been experiencing, and discussing, together.

Moments like these—*friendships* like these—are necessary. They take the sting out of hard things, things like marital bumps in the road (and worse), struggling kids, health scares, failing elders. Things like feeling underappreciated at work, confused about our life's path, or frustrated with the way we look. The intimacy helps us feel less alone. The shared experiences and history, hopefully, help us find the humor in the hard. This stuff just can't happen in the same way online—not even on a screen.

I don't mean to denigrate the potential of internet-based friendships. As someone who's been "very online" for more than a quarter century and who's made multiple lasting friendships there, I know from experience that online acquaintances can develop into strong and intimate relationships. But typically I find it's necessary to break outside the boundaries of the digital world to create those bonds. Telling an internet friend about an experience like my neck-hairdryer collision might have evoked a smile, or even a chuckle—but only *experiencing it with me* had the potential to increase bonding by bringing healing, hysterical laughter to us all.

It's also true that many types of social connections, in addition to close friendships, are important to our mental and emotional health. Spouses make an impact. Siblings make an impact. Children (and, eventually, grandchildren) make an impact. Coworkers, neighbors, and acquaintances make an impact. Even so-called "weak ties"—the connections we create with people we interact with regularly, but not particularly deeply, like the mail carrier, grocery store cashier, or other parents (human or canine) at the park—make an impact. In fact, recent research seems to indicate that experiencing a diversity of different kinds of relationships can play the biggest role in our overall happiness and mental health.

So why, with our lives seemingly more connected than ever, has loneliness become such a problem that Surgeon General Vivek Murthy now calls it an epidemic? It's complex, but Dr. Murthy, and an increasing array of other experts, seems to place a large chunk of the blame squarely on technology itself.

In a world where digital connections are in many cases taking the place of real-life relationships, it's no wonder so many of us feel disconnected and disengaged. Think about it: sharing about our lives—and consuming content about our friends' lives—on social media may *feel* like a real connection...but it's pretty shallow and typically one-sided: nothing like the give-and-take required in sharing stories one-on-one over a beverage.

And we aren't doing so well on the weak-ties front, either, in many ways thanks-no-thanks to technology. When was the last time you went into the bank and chatted with a teller? Do you still go through the regular checkout at the grocery store, or do you opt for an efficient yet impersonal transaction with a computerized self-checkout? Do you even *go* to the store anymore, or are your essentials and not-quite-so essentials mostly being left on your porch by a faceless series of Instacart shoppers and Amazon drivers?

We may think we're gleaning the benefits of close relationships from the internet, but chances are good we're actually getting a pretty poor substitute for actual intimacy. Meanwhile, most of the weak ties people used to experience just going about our business have been usurped by more "convenient" but much less personal processes.

And maybe that's why this internet era is so isolating. It may seem like we're still experiencing the gamut of human social connections, but increasingly they're being facilitated by, filtered through, or simply replaced by digital experiences. As a result, many of us lean a little harder than is healthy on just one or two relationships—a partner, a parent, a child—or perhaps we do the majority of our socializing on the internet. Experts say our emotional health depends on completing a bingo card of diverse social experiences, but increasingly, we're leaving almost all the squares uncovered.

When my aunt's health worsened a couple of weeks after I left, her community rallied around her, offering to take her dog when she was hospitalized and making frequent trips to visit her in the rehab program where she recovered from a stroke suffered during surgery. When she died a few weeks later, her "celebration of life" included an array of friends, some new, some old, people she'd worked to maintain connection with since she was a young woman first arriving in Chicago. I was, once again, struck by the richness of this fiercely independent widow's relationships with friends and family, and it reinforced for me that a love of solitude and a rich social life do not have to be mutually exclusive.

When I consider both my mother and my aunt, and the relationships that supported and sustained their lives, a couple of things stand out to me. First of all, they were from different eras, in which phone calls and in-person get-togethers trumped texts and

Facebook posts as a way of staying in touch. My mother died before social media existed; my aunt stubbornly refused to use it despite having been online since the early '90s.

Without the distraction of hundreds of thousands of "friends" to keep up with, both my mother and my aunt simply stayed in touch with a much more limited number of people, in direct, uncomplicated ways: a phone call, a letter, a lunch date.

I'd be remiss not to mention that Aunt Paula, while offering an open door and soft place to land for her many nieces and nephews plus their children, didn't have children of her own. Her stepson, Bill, lived in a different state growing up, so unlike most women I know, Aunt Paula didn't spend a decade-plus of her life running to ball games and band concerts in the evenings. In other words, her thirties, forties, and fifties weren't defined by the kind of family-focused busyness so many of my friends' lives are today.

But let's be honest: for most of us, that stage—while intense and all-encompassing when it's happening—has a relatively short run. It's convenient and tempting to hide behind our kids as the reason we're too busy to see our nearest and dearest, but at some point most of us will come out the other side ready to reconnect with friends and establish a social life that doesn't revolve around our kids and their activities.

What will we find when we get there?

For myself, I imagine a midlife and, later, an old age defined by real, in-person social connections. And when I look at the old friendships I've held on to and the new ones I've created over the years, I know I owe them the kind of attention that will make that possible. I'm coming out of a stage of life when my family's immediate needs and schedule often take precedence over social opportunities, and that's more than okay. But when that stage has well and truly passed, I need to be ready to make up for lost time.

"But I don't have any close friends," I hear some of you saying. I get it. Friendships don't typically start at the close-and-intimate level (except for a few I made in my twenties at the bathroom sink in the bar; I loved those women intensely for a moment, whoever they were). It takes work and consistency and time, and we can't always control the outcome. If you're starting from scratch in a new town, or perhaps trying to revive your social life after a long period of being head down in motherhood, this part can be *hard*. Not everyone has the good fortune of hanging on to the same friends for decades like I have, and though I am grateful for my two high school besties, those relationships alone can't meet all my social needs.

As is true of most people I know, my social networks are uneven. I'm not always a consistent or reliable friend. I don't always show up the way I could. I often feel too busy giving my attention to hundreds or thousands of connections on a screen to make space for the real people in my real life, even the ones I interact with only briefly.

On social media, the lines between "friend" and "audience" can get blurry, and increasingly it feels like everyone is an influencer, broadcasting more than connecting—myself very much included. And with technology replacing the necessity of so many of the face-to-face transactions we once took for granted, it takes a great deal of intention to add those casual interactions, those "weak ties," back into our lives. But it all matters, and I'm realizing that if I want to live out the rest of my life with a social life that means something, I need to think differently about the role technology plays in my life.

If my mother and my Aunt Paula were still here, I'd love to ask them both how they sustained so many diverse relationships over the years. Then again, I'm pretty sure their answers would be simple: Pick up the phone and call. Schedule the lunch and show up. Do this again and again, and you've built a life in which you've shown other people they matter to you, and in turn, you'll matter to them.

I gotta admit, it sounds a lot better than investing all my friendship energy into Instagram.

Boomer strategies for creating analog relationships in a digital world

No doubt about it, we live in a different world now than our own mothers did at our age. But some things haven't changed—including how much we need connections with other people, both close friendships, and looser ties. Here are some ways to consider building your own personal social net, the analog way:

Write actual letters.

Yes, with a pen. And your hands. And whatever terrible version of your handwriting has survived the last two decades of digital-forward communication. In the modern, machine-driven age, when you don't even need to text your own thoughts anymore (there's AI for that, after all), there's something truly revolutionary-feeling about putting pen to paper and slowly scratching out a personal message. And that's why it's so special: think how excited you'd be to get a piece of real, handwritten mail in your box! Writing handwritten letters is a practice I committed to earlier this year, and it really has changed the way I think about staying in touch (as well as the things I share, and the way and reasons I share them). For inspiration and a solid plan to help you get started, check out the books *The Thank-You Project: Cultivating Happiness One Letter of Gratitude at a Time,* by my friend Nancy Davis Kho, and *Please Write: Finding Joy and Meaning in the Soulful Art of Handwritten Letters,* by Lynne M. Kolze.

Choose in-person experiences.

Yes, you can find workout videos online, but why not show up for an in-real-life yoga class every now and then? And while I've become just as dependent on self-checkout as the next person (thank you, corporate overlords!), lately I've been making a point to go through the regular checkout and make a friendly, human connection with the cashier. Not every time, mind you—but enough to feel like I'm still engaging in the traditional human pleasantries that make communities work.

Go deep.

It's not always easy to go beyond small talk in this stage of life, even with your closest friends. From marriage growing pains to big big-kid problems to potentially embarrassing health issues, midlife can bring things that are just hard to talk about. And because it's hard for everyone, you might have to take it upon yourself to go first and set the tone. The book *Share Your Stuff. I'll Go First.* by Laura Tremaine provides a hefty dose of encouragement plus some solid strategies for being the one who "goes first" in starting conversations that search deep, strengthen bonds, and slay loneliness.

OUR HORMONES, OURSELVES:

THE OPPORTUNITY OF PERIMENOPAUSE

---

ike most other Gen X women, I first became aware of hormones in the fourth grade, when on one momentous day the teachers separated the girls and boys and proceeded to tell the girls how, one day soon, hormones would overtake our bodies, turning us from the carefree girls we were perfectly happy being into temperamental, hairy, rounded, bleeding strangers.

As a young-for-my-age eight-year-old who still played daily with dolls and My Little Pony, everything about this scenario horrified me. As it turned out, I needn't have worried: by the time my breasts finally showed up four years later, and my period the year after that, I'd been waiting so long I was more bored and impatient than nervous.

Still, at that point, while I had a fuzzy understanding that "hormones" were responsible for my development, my pubic hair, and my period—and were also perhaps part of the reason I often wanted to punch my mother square in the face—they mostly existed for me as a vague concept. It wasn't until I was pregnant with my oldest son that I dived deep into the physical mysteries of the female body, reading every book I could get my hands on about ovulation, conception, pregnancy, birth, postpartum, lactation—and the role of hormones in each of these processes.

I began to understand more fully just how a unique cocktail of hormones dictates not only what happens to our bodies, but often how we feel about what's happening. With five pregnancies and births, long periods of breastfeeding, and the hills and valleys between, I had plenty of material to draw on: basically, I'd become a walking science-fair experiment on the hormones of fertility and motherhood. I was fascinated by it all: how pregnancy hormones communicated with my body to help keep a developing baby *in*, and how, at just the right time, another hormone would signal to my body that it was time to get the baby *out*. How hormones would help my body know when it was time to produce milk—and not only when, but also *what quality* of milk and how much of it my baby needed. And, most fascinating to me, how the hormone oxytocin played a crucial role in helping me bond with my baby, staying in that warm-and-fuzzy, nurturing emotional place to keep each one safe, fed, and warm long enough to make it to a more independent state.

From what happened to my body during each stage of fertility to how I fed, and felt about, my baby, it seemed that hormones controlled everything about my life.

And now, in the midst of perimenopause, it seems they still do.

"During menopause, a woman can feel like the only way she

can continue to exist for 10 more seconds inside her crawling, burning skin is to walk screaming into the sea—grandly, epically, and terrifyingly, like a 15-foot-tall Greek tragic figure wearing a giant, pop-eyed wooden mask," wrote the comedian Sandra Tsing Loh in a story for *The Atlantic* in 2011. I remember older friends of mine sharing the story when it was published, and I found it amusing and well written—but at the age of thirty-four, and still two years away from the hysterectomy that would definitively end my fertile period, I didn't think that it held much meaning for me.

But when I stumbled across the story again a few months ago, it made a much bigger impact. Especially this part:

> ...*as the female body's egg-producing abilities and levels of estrogen and other reproductive hormones begin to wane, so does the hormonal cloud of our nurturing instincts. During this huge biological shift, our brain, temperament, and behaviors will begin to change—as then must, alarmingly, our relationships.*

The chemical changes associated with perimenopause include dips in levels of oxytocin, the same hormone that once brought me to tears over love for my baby. As levels of estrogen lower, so does oxytocin, experts explain, which can make us feel less tolerant of our families and less willing to sacrifice for them. Even if a woman grew her family via adoption or another means besides personally growing and delivering a baby, she will have been in this same hormonal fog during what are referred to as "the childbearing years."

Those hormonal changes are why it's theorized that women

become less focused on others, and more focused on themselves, as they enter perimenopause. All of which could explain, in part, the drastic turn my life took in my mid- to late thirties.

With my brain awash in oxytocin during the arms-full stage of motherhood, I had been chemically primed to nurture and sacrifice. For years, my biological imperative inspired me to sacrifice for my children to keep them alive...and oxytocin helped me feel pretty good about that self-sacrifice most of the time. But that hormone-induced selflessness often didn't stop at my baby; instead, the drive to caretake benefited my entire family and often spilled beyond the borders of my own home, as well.

A mother's brain chemistry propels her to give and give and give—until, at some point, whether due to the gradual natural process of perimenopause or a more abrupt change that might accompany illness or surgery, that chemistry shifts. Suddenly, the theory posits, she sees the unfairness of her burden and decides she's *over it.*

The fallout can be dramatic. Most of us have heard stories about women burning it all down in their perimenopausal years: blowing up careers, marriages, friendships, family-of-origin dynamics. An internet search of "perimenopause rage" brings up an interesting mix of results: most of the articles seem to blame fluctuating emotions squarely on hormones, and the "cure" seems to come from finding ways to balance those hormones, whether with diet, exercise, sleep, supplements, hormone replacement therapy (HRT), lifestyle changes, or the simple but frustrating act of waiting it out.

Over the years I've read many clinical assessments of what's happening to our bodies and minds during the perimenopausal process, with concrete, evidence-based suggestions of how to help us cope as we ride it out. I find the suggestions interesting and somewhat helpful, but this "just the facts" approach often leaves me cold. To me it's evident there is so much more going on than simply hot flashes and a stone-cold sex drive.

Dig a little deeper, and you'll find other schools of thought surrounding just what this period of time, and our accompanying emotions, really represents. In Sharon Blackie's wonderful book *Hagitude: Reimagining the Second Half of Life*, she writes extensively about these changes to our bodies, brains, and feelings through the lens of fairy-tale archetypes. "Menopause, like all times of transition, is a time between stories, when the old story fades and a new story is waiting to emerge," she writes. "During this period of intense physical change, it's almost necessary to turn inward, to embark upon the inner work of elderhood—the work of reimagining and shaping who we want to be in the world, of gaining new perspectives on life, of challenging and evolving our belief systems, of exploring our calling, of uncovering meaning, and ultimately finding healing for a lifetime's accumulation of wounds."

Authors who take a more holistic view of the perimenopausal period, like Blackie, don't discount the biological reality of hormonal shifts—they simply argue that there may be a meaning and purpose to the emotions and chaos they can unleash and that perhaps we would do ourselves a favor by leaning into those emotions a little to discover their purpose and potential (rather than immediately rushing to cover them up so we can return to a calmer and more socially palatable version of ourselves).

In her *Atlantic* piece, Tsing Loh presents an alternate view to the common idea that menopause is the "change" of life. In her view, the selflessness of our fertile years—*not* the comparative self-centeredness of our post-fertile years—is the aberration that requires explanation:

> ...*it is not menopause that triggers the mind-altering and hormone-altering variation; the hormonal "disturbance" is actually fertility. Fertility is The Change. It is during fertility that a female loses herself, and enters that cloud overly rich in estrogen. And of course, simply chronologically speaking, over the whole span of her life, the self-abnegation that fertility induces is not the norm—the more standard state of selfishness is.*

Perhaps she's right. And yet, I have to believe that it's all a matter of degree. While it sounds novel—and probably very restful—to face a life directed purely by self-interests, in the end it doesn't feel any more desirable to me than a life spent in martyrdom only to the interests of others. While my life has gone through a recalibration over the past ten years, I actually found myself coming back to some sort of center after the extreme self-focus of the years surrounding my divorce. Perhaps, like other phases, that one was necessary—but only for a short time. Perhaps now, as the size of my household dwindles, it creates a sort of expansiveness within me to think more globally about the ways I can nurture people besides my immediate family.

Including myself.

Mothers have valid reason to mourn the passing of our child-bearing years. Even if we are completely satisfied with our family size, it's normal to feel intense nostalgia for a period of life we'd never choose to return to. Culturally there is so much tied up in what it means to be young and fertile, and our last gasps of fertility can feel like a line of demarcation between our youth and what we're afraid may lie on the other side of menopause: Will we still feel relevant? Vital? Energetic? Valuable? Alive?

I've been trying to remind myself that, of the eight-plus decades of life an average female can expect to live these days, most of us spend a very short window of that time actually making babies. I was alive for thirteen years before I became fertile, and another seven before my body created a baby. Sixteen years and five babies later, that window, for me, had closed permanently. I crammed a lot of baby making into that short window, and yet I still have so much creative potential to explore: decades and decades to play, to love, to nurture, to explore, to learn, to imagine.

How I spend the years I have left—and how I *feel* about the way I spend them—may be influenced by the particular mix of hormones coursing through my body at any given time, but I'm not willing to believe that I'm entirely at their mercy. Oxytocin and estrogen, the hormones that dominated my personal chemical cocktail in early motherhood, may have helped me bond with my newborns, but they didn't automatically turn me into a nurturing earth mother. Neither will their decline automatically turn me into a bitter swamp witch.

Like most modern women, I've spent a lifetime internalizing cultural messages that women matter only when we're objects of sexual desire, while we're reproducing or raising offspring, or both. I'd spent over a decade and a half writing one kind of story, only to see it come to an abrupt close—without a clear plotline in sight for the rest of my life. At some point, we all find ourselves standing in that uncertain place, without a lot of inspiration to draw from our cultural view of aging. No wonder the identity shift that happens to moms in midlife—myself included—can be so hard to cope with.

"Finding our path through this time between stories that menopause represents, and feeling our way into whatever story might be offering itself to us next, is complicated by the fact that we're not educated to expect that elderhood might offer up a new story at all," Blackie writes in *Hagitude*. "If Western culture teaches us anything about elderhood, it's that it's supposed to mark the end of all meaningful stories, not the beginning of a new one. But there can be a certain perverse pleasure, as well as a sense of rightness and beauty, in insisting on flowering just when the world expects you to become quiet and diminish."

As a young mother, I took the tendency toward nurturing that nature had given me and, through effort and determination, helped it make me an attentive mother. But now, as I move into a phase where those hormones no longer make caretaking quite so automatic, I'm free to write a new story. For me, caretaking will likely always be part of my life. But it's exciting to be able to look up and out from the little family unit that absorbed my energy for so long and to see a future in which I can finally turn some of that nurturing energy inward toward myself—and outward as well, in service of the wider world.

CREATIVITY:

THE NEW FERTILITY

Despite the ever-shrinking number of inhabitants in my home, my kitchen is nonetheless currently teeming with life: bacterial life, to be specific. Last year—decades after I began nurturing some serious homesteader fantasies that, alas, never came to fruition in the younger years of my life—I crossed a life goal off my list: I milked a friend's goat and brought home several quarts of raw milk.

Since then, my kitchen has been a living laboratory, with jars of milk in various stages of fermentation. So far I've made tangy yogurt, fresh chèvre, a passable mozzarella, and several jars of creamy clabber, a simple ferment that can serve as a starting point for multiple other dairy products. More challenging aged cheeses are surely in my future: cheddar, Gouda, perhaps Brie?

Working with raw milk has required a mindset shift that hasn't been easy for someone like me, raised in the decades after food safety became synonymous with high-temperature treatment and various other scientific preservation processes.

Most of us are familiar with pasteurized milk, which has been heated to kill off bacteria—both the kind that can make you sick in certain circumstances and the kind that can be cultivated to create delicious cheese, yogurt, and the various other fermented dairy products that have been the way agrarian societies have preserved milk for thousands of years. When working with pasteurized milk, a cheesemaker's job is to add back the right kind and proportion of bacterial cultures and then create the right conditions for those bacteria to reestablish themselves upon what is essentially a blank slate.

When you're working with raw milk, however, it's more about standing back and letting the bacteria that are already present do their thing. In both cases, the creative task is essentially to guide and facilitate the process of bacterial life in doing what it does, in order to create a delicious and less perishable fermented product. Cheese, it turns out, is quite a fecund and fertile thing.

I've been thinking a lot about the link between creativity, cheese, and fertility lately—partly because I've been spending a lot of time attempting to understand the reproductive processes that are present as part of the fermentation process and partly because no longer having small children of my own opens up my kitchen for these kinds of projects, and my time and brain space for uninterrupted musing.

Learning a new process takes me a long time and a lot of trial and error. I'm bad at following recipes and slow to understand cause and effect. I'm also forgetful and highly distractible even on my best, most focused days. Projects requiring frequently checking in on a starter, maintaining a consistent temperature over an extended period of time, or a patient wait-and-see approach proved more than I could handle during that intense period where I was already prone to burning brown-and-serve rolls.

Sure, I cooked plenty in those days, but it was mostly forgiving, tried-and-true food like baked pasta or low-and-slow pot roasts that could hang out in the oven an extra thirty minutes or more without dire effect if I forgot to set a timer (I *always* forget to set a timer). Back then, I simply didn't have the mental space to internalize touchy multistep processes, or the patience to try, and try, and try again—so more ambitious projects like sourdough baking or soap making seemed always elusive.

Now I'm learning a new way of being in the kitchen—one in which the main goal isn't to get in, get food made, and get back out as quickly as possible, but one in which I can linger, make mistakes, and take pleasure in the process. *You have time,* I keep having to remind myself when frustrated by an undesired result; *You have so much time.* Time to create, to play, to express my fertile creative power—ironically, much more deeply than I could do when I was actually fertile.

When I had my hysterectomy, my kids ranged in age from four to fifteen. I'll admit, after a decade and a half of living in service to my body's fecundity, there was no small sense of relief in having the possibility of pregnancy permanently taken off the table.

But there was grief, too. My surgery marked an abrupt, no-going-back end to the thing that had most defined my twenties and early thirties: fertility. Those milk-soaked years of early motherhood would be missed and mourned, I knew, even if leaving them behind was in my best interests on multiple levels.

A month or two after my surgery, I found myself daydreaming

up a book idea about a possible dystopian future in which an alien race had taken over with the intent to breed with humans and create a half-human, half-alien race. I mused that a woman like me might be able to escape slaughter if the aliens believed me to be a fertile woman, and I wondered how long it would take them to figure out that I was not capable of bearing children and exterminate me.

While I vaguely considered that becoming a breed slave for an evil alien race—kept alive only to birth alien-human hybrid babies to populate the planet in a sort of *Handmaid's Tale/Independence Day* mash-up—isn't exactly better than just being killed off from the get-go, "*At least you'd still have value to society,*" whispered some small voice in the dark recesses of my reptilian brain.

I never wrote down a single word of the story. Maybe I just didn't want to play out how it might end for the character based on the no-longer-fertile woman whose entire value was wrapped up in reproduction. And yet, the fact that I had the daydream at all speaks to messages I've absorbed about what my ability to bear children—a lot of them in a short time—meant about my value then and what losing that ability meant about how I perceived my value going forward.

While my surgery effectively ended my childbearing years forever, as a still relatively young woman with a passel of little kids following me wherever I went, I could still pass—even though I technically was not—for years. Strangely, retaining the outward appearance of that identity brought me some comfort. If you'd asked me point-blank, of course I would have denied that I felt that way. Yet here I was, on some level grateful that the world wouldn't know from looking at me that I was no longer able to reproduce.

The finality of it all is starting to catch up with me, though. At forty-seven, I'm finally past the stage where I can easily pass for a woman who could get knocked up without too much trouble—and that means I have to accept that it's been quite some time since that was my reality. There are all kinds of feelings tied up with that, most of which have nothing to do with my actual level desire to make more babies—which these days is pretty close to zero—and more to do with the loss of identity, of purpose, of societal value that goes along with being a young woman who is still perceived as fertile.

I sometimes find myself fixating on my missing period and what it might be able to tell me about where I am in my theoretical fertility cycle. Without a period, how will I know when I've crossed the line into menopause and have finally put that fertility behind me? *Who cares, anyway?* Well, as embarrassing as it feels to admit, apparently I do.

Here's the truth, though: for all intents and purposes, I am no longer a fertile woman, and I haven't been for more than a decade. The stage of life in which I created and birthed and nursed children of my own is long in my rear-view mirror. There is a real loss there, and it would be dishonest to dismiss it. And yet, while I look back on that belly-full, breasts-full, arms-full stage with much tender nostalgia, I have no real desire to go back.

And over the past decade-plus, that period of my life has given way to a new kind of fertility. The years since I lost the ability to bear children have been full of creative expression for me. I rediscovered performance, acting and singing in multiple plays and concerts. I birthed a business with Sarah, my partner at Mom Hour Media. After my divorce, I summoned all my creative energy to manifest an entirely new way of living for myself and my children. I have helped each of those children to take steps toward their own visions for young adulthood. I fed and nurtured a new relationship, and my now-husband, Eric, and I created an entirely new marriage… so different from my first that it hardly seems like the same institution. Together he and I have created multiple businesses as well, including a retail market we opened with my sister and brother-in-law in northern Michigan. I started Bevy, a brick-and-mortar tea shop. And now, as I putter around my new kitchen making cheese, surrounded by a new family formed out of the slightly singed pieces of the old one, I'm slowly beginning to realize the creative dreams of my young self, the girl whose early dreams held such clarity and promise.

But we can find new ways to channel that creative energy and find new purpose. Over the last few years I've talked with many women in their forties and beyond: in real life among my close friends, at the retreats I've facilitated, and in my online community. One of my favorite things to witness has been the blossoming realization that creativity is not just a thing for "artsy types" and that it also doesn't require an end goal or product. Creativity, in its essence, is a vibrant energy source we can all tap into.

In early motherhood, that creative energy was usurped by the incredible amount of creativity it took to parent. Think about the voices you invented for the characters in the board books you read to your infant; the little games and stories you made up for your toddler. Consider the creative skills necessary to get a resistant child excited about (or at least compliant with) a trip to the beach or zoo or to keep two squalling siblings from ruining a road trip for the whole family. Even the most basic meal planning is a creative act. So is calendar planning. At its most essential, creativity is simply a process using the imagination—and early motherhood requires a lot of it.

The beautiful thing is that, as our kids get older, parenting them requires a little less of this sort of hands-on, in-the-moment creative energy. Which leaves so much more available for projects we really want to work on. It is, I think, why you see so many women in middle age take up new creative pursuits. We teach yoga or breed dogs, make sourdough bread or pick up a paintbrush for the first time since eighth grade.

The objects of my creative focus have shifted, it's true. The dream of a cozy, bustling family home filled with babies is behind me, and I do miss both its sweet simplicity and its frenetic energy at times. But now, surrounded by activity of another sort, with many years of exploration stretching out in front of me, I've never felt more creative.

In this phase of life, it turns out, I'm standing on very fertile ground indeed.

THREE RESOURCES TO HELP YOU TAP INTO YOUR CREATIVITY

If you've decided to embrace your creative side, it can help to have a few inspiring resources to help get you going. Here are a few places to start:

1. *Big Magic: Creative Living Beyond Fear,* by Elizabeth Gilbert.

   This book has it all: no-nonsense advice on living a creative life from a bestselling and prolific author with just the right-size dose of woo-woo to help you see the magical possibility in creative pursuits.

2. *The Artist's Way* **by Julia Cameron.**

This book is a classic for a reason: it's what helped me feel empowered enough to embrace creativity decades ago, and even today, when I'm feeling stuck, I find myself flipping through its pages.

3. The Internet

The Internet is a great way to meet and connect with other people who are leaning into their innate creativity and who'd love to take you along on the journey. Lately I've been leaning into the creative community I've found on Substack, where I host regular events like Co-Create Workshops in which participants work on a variety of creative projects from painting to stitching to writing to organizing their recipes (head to my site, meaganfrancis.com, to learn more); and I also follow multiple creators who inspire me across a variety of media, from illustration to writing to kitchen craft.

ON CHICKENS, CHILDREN, AND CHOOSING CARETAKING

don't get it. Your kids are finally getting old enough to be self-sufficient, and some of them are starting to move out. Why would you want to add more things to take care of?"

My friend Candice had a point. Over a happy-hour drink I'd just told her about the twenty-four—yes, *twenty-four*—fluffy balls of living baby chicken I'd just acquired in a feverish feed-store chick-binge.

A few months earlier the kids and I had moved onto several acres, right around the corner from Eric. Our relationship was slowly but steadily heading toward marriage as our lives simplified: when we'd met, he still had two kids at home and I had three, with the oldest two still making frequent lengthy returns to the nest. Two years later, the number of minors under our collective roofs had been slashed in half, and in four years, we'd both have empty nests. Moving to a home within walking distance of his was a sort of transitional move before jumping into the deep end of commitment and cohabitation, and the house's country location was a significant move in the direction I saw my life moving in.

With both of his kids now out in the world and my active parenting years quickly evaporating, our five-year plans had started to take on a tinge of fantasy: we could live full-time in a renovated school bus! Or on a sailboat! Or a cruise ship! Or in Europe! After decades of suppressing wanderlust, of feeling rooted by the responsibilities of a family, the idea of being able to get up and go anywhere—without answering to anyone about it—was temporarily intoxicating.

But instead of beginning the process of shedding my ties to other creatures so that, once Clara had graduated, I'd be ready to fly, I'd just gone and tethered myself to twenty-four needy little chicks.

I can't remember when it was that I became enamored with the idea of chickens. Maybe always. It was an idle sort of dream, though, as I'd spent the majority of my adult life living in municipalities that didn't allow backyard poultry. I remember reading a story about an enterprising preteen girl who fought city hall for her right to keep a backyard flock...and lost. I shook my head and cluck-clucked at the injustice, and I entertained some vague fantasies about having chickens myself one day. But as I also lived within that fated, authoritarian zip code, my fantasies were safe from any responsibility to act them out.

But now that we lived on acreage, it seemed that all possible barriers had been eliminated. Eric himself had laid the trap by taking me to the farm-supply store during "chick days." I'd look down at the little balls of fluff peep-peeping their way around their clear plastic tubs and desperately want to take some home. But in the back of my mind I felt a little panicky about the whole thing. It all seemed too easy. I could buy live birds at the same store where they sell garden rakes and Carhartt? And then take said living creatures home? Isn't there, like, an application process? Don't they know I have no idea what I'm doing?

After a few trips to browse, watching other normal-seeming people walk out with their own hatchlings, I started to feel more confident—and desperate. If I didn't get myself some chicks soon, I worried I'd miss my chance entirely.

I now know better, of course. One only has to walk through a feed store at any time of the spring or summer to know that baby chicks aren't exactly a rare commodity. But my longing to acquire them was intense: stronger than my idle fantasy of living on a boat, or in a bus, or even traveling to Europe. So one day we returned—with my daughter Clara and Eric's daughter Sammi in tow—with the intent of choosing a handful of chicks to take home.

I'd read about a concept called "chicken math" among homesteaders and backyard chicken raisers alike. From what I can make out, chicken math simply means the tendency for our best-laid chicken plans to career wildly out of scope. It works like this: you intend to get four chicks, but the feed store offers to discount the price if you take eight. Or you go in looking for a certain breed and walk out with that breed and their brooder-mates, plus two others you didn't even know you needed—but those teeny cheep-cheeps and fuzzy feathers were just too cute to pass up.

Now, I was facing my own "chicken math." Initially I thought six or eight pullets (female chicks, which will grow up into hens) would be a perfectly reasonable number for a newbie to take on. But as I researched breeds and care, my thinking became more expansive. The six acres my family's new home sat on seemed impossibly large after a lifetime of living on city lots. Eric had promised to build a roomy coop. We had a large fenced area where they could safely roam. Why stop at ten? My property could probably fit hundreds, I figured.

Or dozens, anyway, which is what I actually wound up with.

It all happened in a blur. I walked in planning to buy only Jersey Giants and Rhode Island Reds. I'd read that they were hardy and good layers, easy starter chickens that I could learn on and add to the flock once I'd gotten my feet under me. I planned to get three of each.

But as the sales associate scooped them up one by one into the box, I found myself feverishly exhorting her to add one more, one more; *this one, that one hiding in the corner, she's too cute to leave behind.* Now we were at twelve—a good place to stop, right?

But those creamy-yellow Brahmas one brooder over! There were just three left, and a quick Google search told me they'd grow into lovable, docile, feathery-footed giants. I pointed at the Brahmas, and the associate plucked the unsuspecting chicks from their temporary home, put them in the box, then closed it and handed it to me.

I staggered a little under its shifting, feathery weight; the responsibility of all those fragile little bodies tempered by an intoxicating vision of adult hens waddling around our yard eating bugs, clucking contentedly, fresh eggs for our morning breakfasts…

Sensing my disorientation, the associate leaned in for the kill shot. "I'll give you a dollar off the Bantams if you take them all," she said conspiratorially, gesturing to another brooder full of wee striped things running in circles around one another. They seemed older than the others, except that they were so tiny. Nine of them. My addled brain tried to do the "chicken math," but I had lost all ability to perform basic arithmetic. I nodded numbly as she popped open another box. It wasn't until I was standing at the register that I was able to figure out my math.

The chicks stayed in a box for a few weeks and then took over a corner room in our shop building while their coop was being built and the weather was warming up enough to let them roam outside. When they were small and too slow to get away, we'd scoop them up and cuddle them. But as they got older, I began to feel decidedly overwhelmed. They started getting smart and fast enough to dodge a human hand, and even if I managed to identify one or two that were less skittish and seemed like pet material, they all looked exactly alike to me, so I'd lose track of which was which. In the end, there were just too many chicks to turn any of them into pets, so I simply let them be chickens.

In my fervor, I'd also failed to notice that the sign in the Bantam brooder had indicated a "straight run," meaning those chicks had not been divided by sex—which became evident as they grew. Of the nine "hens," four actually turned out to be roosters. Six roosters to fourteen hens is not good chicken math for a variety of reasons and led to stressed-out hens and a constant cacophony of crowing from the yard. By early summer two of the roosters were "culled," which is a nice way of saying slaughtered. Eric plucked and cleaned their tiny bodies, and I carefully seasoned, roasted, and served them, suddenly so very aware of the many birds that had been delivered to me on Styrofoam under plastic on a supermarket shelf, then had been wasted when I'd forgotten about them until their sell-by date had passed. These little guys, still sporting a few tiny pinfeathers, had just a day ago been strutting around my backyard, yelling at me from the top of the fence if I approached their ladies. They had hardly any meat on their bones, but it seemed shameful not to pick them clean.

Of the remaining Bantams, most of them turned out to be prison breakers, flying in and out of the yard at will. They enjoyed one glorious summer free-ranging around the yard by day without consequences and returning to the coop before dark to nest down for the night with the others. But in the fall, we lost most of the Bantam hens over a matter of days. We didn't witness any drama, just noticed that suddenly there were a lot fewer hens going in and out of the nesting boxes in the morning. What happened is hard to say. A predator may have been lurking around the chicken yard, picking off the easy kills on the outside of the fence but not interested in messing around with the much bigger chickens huddled together inside, or the Bantam hens may have gotten bold and wandered too far away, right into enemy territory. Either way, that particular session of nature's culling seemed to have ended with the Bantams. I was grateful I hadn't gotten too attached.

Of course, I couldn't have known how all of this would turn out that day when my friend Candice posed that question to me over our glasses of wine. Why would I, a mother who'd put in over two decades of intensive work tending to the daily physical, mental, and emotional needs of five human beings, and who finally found herself coming to the end of the bulk of that work, willingly and intentionally add more hassle to her life?

It was a completely reasonable question, after all. Candice's daughter is still young; simply getting out for a happy hour requires logistical planning and tag-teaming with her spouse. When she returned home from our outing, there would still be parenting to do. I remember well the feeling of oppression that can come from so much being needed.

But now I've experienced a taste of what's on the other side of it, as well. A divorce with a fifty-fifty parenting time split when my kids were mostly still young created an abrupt transition to long periods of time in an empty house: no one raiding the snack basket, slamming doors, or leaving sticky dishes in the sink. The side of me that prefers solitude and tidiness, that revels in doing precisely what I want when I want, quite liked this weightless feeling of freedom, the hours open and fluid instead of shaped by other people's needs. As my kids got older and one by one left home, my life has more and more followed the fluid path of freedom. Yet the side of me that knows what it means to give part of yourself up for another being remains. And, it turns out, that side of me hasn't been so easy to walk away from.

In my early, arms-full days of mothering, on more than one occasion I fantasized about running away from it all: the endless diapers and feedings and nights spent walking the floor, all the expectations and monotony and noise and mess. Sometimes it felt like being caged or like my skin was crawling, like I could climb the walls. Other days, the longing for freedom was more akin to a dull, throbbing ache.

But these days it's hard to replicate either of those feelings. I am faced with long, childless hours of quiet and freedom when Clara's with her dad or off at school. When she's home, I have to bribe and beckon and lure her to me. Long gone are the days when small children literally climbed over my body as I tried to work, read, or nap; now that Clara's left to her own devices, we could go days without interacting much. It's disquieting to realize not only how available freedom has become to me, but also how ill-prepared I am to use it.

I spent my kids' childhoods creating a cozy and comfortable coop for all of us, and I now find that I quite like being inside it. In just a few years, I could fly away without any legal or moral or societal repercussions. But now that that's true, I'm having a hard time summoning enough fervor to take flight.

There are so many ways I could spend the next several decades of my life, and there's a part of me that is tempted to shake off the rooting force of being needed. I've been there, done that, after all, and I deserve to be a little selfish, right? It's time to do things for *me* now, to take care of what *I* want. And yes, that does sound nice, and necessary, to a certain degree.

And yet, "I guess I just like taking care of things," I found myself saying to Candice in response to her question about the chickens. It seemed like a lame, sappy thing to say, as a mother who'd already given two and a half decades to "taking care of things" and was finally facing a chance to live it up a little. But for me it's true.

Mothers are constantly hearing about the dangers of "losing ourselves" in motherhood, which never made a lot of sense to me in my arms-full years. That loss of self felt normal and even necessary in the early years, a yielding and surrender to my new reality that had to happen for me to find peace and happiness in it instead of fighting it all the time. I can see how that surrender could take on a different, sadder sort of flavor if, while those same kids were engaged in their rapid exit from my family home, I couldn't think of a single thing I wanted to do for myself, if I couldn't imagine a life after motherhood.

But what if the life I imagine for myself post-motherhood takes me at my best, taps into that well of life-giving energy I learned to harness while nurturing and nourishing children, and simply redirects it?

Sarah and I have often joked on *The Mom Hour* about "midlife lady leisure pursuits"; about the hobbies and pastimes women start to be drawn to as their kids age. Sometimes they're individual, self-oriented activities: running or painting or Pilates. But just as often, they include care and nurturing. Starting a garden or fostering kittens or volunteering at a women's shelter. Breeding puppies or starting a book club. It seems many of us, when we reach midlife, are not looking to excuse ourselves from caregiving. Youth taught us to desire flight, freedom, irresponsibility. But perhaps age is teaching us the value of staying put and tending.

Over the past eight years, I've had enough breaks from caretaking to realize that I'm actually not happiest when completely left to my own devices and desires. Family, or a community, or living creatures whose needs I am responsible for meeting...all can act as grounding and stabilizing anchors to a life that needs rootedness more than I might always want to acknowledge when other people and their endless needs are getting on my nerves.

As a mother in the arms-full stage, I didn't have much choice about whether I showed up for my kids every day. In this new stage of life, yes! I have a choice, and the chance to rekindle parts of my creativity that lay dormant, fulfill needs that were unmet, and become reacquainted with parts of me that went unexplored for decades. It's a worthy and valuable pursuit, focusing time and energy on myself and my own needs. And yet, among all this turning inward, all this choosing of myself, I find myself with one hand facing out, palm up, open to receiving and meeting the needs of others, too. Not all of the others, and not all of the time, but someone, and sometimes.

In this stage of life, God willing, I have enough time left to choose a lot of things. Maybe one day I'll still choose life on a sailboat, or in a school bus, or in Scotland or Spain. Perhaps there are other adventures ahead of me I can't imagine just yet.

But right now? I choose chickens.

THE
GRANDMOTHER
HYPOTHESIS

———————

wanted to be a good mother, that's all—" begins the chapter titled "A Mother's Work" in Robin Wall Kimmerer's fantastic book, *Braiding Sweetgrass: Indigenous Wisdom, Scientific Knowledge and the Teachings of Plants.* When I got to the end of the chapter I cried, then immediately went back and reread it from the beginning. The chapter begins with Kimmerer impulsively buying her young daughters ducklings at the feed store, then realizing the growing ducklings are turning the pond into a thick, algae-covered soup.

Now, in order to be a good mother, she must clear the pond of the algae she helped create...by wanting to be a good mother. Grappling with complicated feelings about this—is putting so much effort into something that only serves her two children actually selfish in the face of larger need? Will any of it matter anyway, once they have grown and gone?—Kimmerer poignantly realizes the expansive nature and scope of the work we do in the private spheres of our own homes. In the end, Kimmerer muses, the "good mothering" we provide our families *does* matter to the greater whole: "What I do here matters. Everyone lives downstream. My pond drains to the brook, to the creek, to a great and needful lake. The water net connects us all," she writes.

The hopeful message in Kimmerer's words is that motherhood isn't just a snapshot in time or a blip that ends once our kids leave home. In real and significant ways, we continue on in our role of "mother"—and in fact, that role takes on even more significance: "I have shed tears into that flow when I thought that motherhood would end. But the pond has shown me that being a good mother doesn't end with creating a home where just my children can flourish. A good mother grows into a richly eutrophic old woman, knowing that her work doesn't end until she creates a home where all of life's beings can flourish."

A few years back I became aware of the "grandmother hypothesis," an explanation for why women, on average, outlive their fertile period by many decades. The hypothesis states that the presence of a living grandmother has a protective effect on future generations, helping children to survive and mothers to have more babies in a shorter period of time.

This hypothesis has been challenged and is far from universally accepted. But I suspect that, like me, many mothers in midlife would like to believe it's true. The alternative—that we are somehow used up and even useless once we are no longer capable of creating new life—is an easy idea to internalize, even if logically we know it's an absolutely garbage way to think about ourselves as human beings. The "grandmother hypothesis" gives us a new lens through which to consider our value and role as we age, even for those who didn't have children to begin with.

Of course, that all assumes that our value—in fact, our essential nature, our reason for being here at all—is tied up in being of service to others. After so many years caregiving and self-sacrifice, I know well how easy it is to bristle at the thought: "Oh, great, I took care of people for decades, and now that they're finally grown and gone, it turns out my future role is to *keep taking care of people?*"

But isn't that what we're all here for, when we really get down to basics: to take care of one another? Maybe we've gotten it all wrong, trying to compartmentalize our lives so much. The formula of American life that's been marketed to us seems to be bookended with an independent, self-serving youth and an independent, self-serving older age at either end as well as a lifetime's worth of caretaking crammed into a couple of decades in the middle.

Don't get me wrong: I have no desire to go back to the sleepless nights of early parenthood. I did my time and then some in that stage already. But when I look a little more expansively at what it might look like to be a "good mother"—to create a home, to nurture life, to take care of people—in this next stage, the idea of what my purpose looks like now seems to take on new life.

I can't control whether my kids decide to bless me with a dozen grandchildren, though I hope they will. But here's what I like about the "grandmother hypothesis": it reminds me that I still have an important role to play in the thriving of my community and in the forming and flourishing of new families—maybe primarily by helping it seem possible to start them in the first place.

Young people in the Western world aren't very keen to reproduce at the moment, and that trend will have some major ramifications sooner than we might be aware of: the United Nations predicts that, in the United States, the annual birth rate will be eclipsed by the annual death rate in 2043, and a Bradley Intelligence Report on this trend says we will begin feeling the impacts of "this ticking demographic time bomb" long before that date. Underpopulation is a real problem and one we're likely to feel the pressures of in our own old age.

But as a mother of five, I'm not interested in a world where people have kids just because they feel obligated to keep my cohorts' Social Security going. At the end of the day, I want people to *want* to have kids.

Not *all* people, of course. There have always been, and will always be, people for whom parenting isn't the right path. But right now, the number of people who feel that parenting is not for them is historically unprecedented. In a 2021 Pew report, 44 percent of nonparents younger than fifty said they were unlikely to ever have children. *Forty-four percent.* The fact that parenting seems impossible (or unpalatable) to such a large percentage of our young people should be a huge, blinking red light telling us that we are getting a lot of things wrong.

I don't think everyone should have kids. But I still want some people, *many* people, to desire this life I've lived, to see the possibility and joy in it, much the same way a math teacher or poet or dentist might get excited when young people decide to follow in their footsteps. I've devoted most of my adulthood and much of my career to the exploration of motherhood as a role, a relationship, and an identity. I know that it can be both unbelievably difficult but also surprisingly rewarding. I know it requires—and sharpens—skills and smarts. I know it's the most important work I've ever done.

And I also know that right now, we are massively failing at creating a world where it looks that way.

I'm not just talking about the culture-changing anxiety of living in the shadow of a poorly managed global pandemic, the mess of an economic reality young people are trying to grapple with right now, or the ecological disasters that threaten to turn our planet into a smoldering swamp. Sickness and sky-high inflation, extreme weather, and other existential threats have been a reality throughout history, and people have kept having babies.

And while many books have been written about the organizational changes that would help make working parenthood more sustainable, we don't talk nearly as much about the things regular people, particularly the older generation of regular people, can do. What if we took the lead on modeling a healthy, balanced approach to parenting, supporting young parents and young people who want to become parents, and creating a more family-friendly world?

I want, one day, to be surrounded by healthy, happy, safe grandbabies and other people's grandbabies. But just as important, I want those grandbabies to come from parents who are enjoying raising them and are glad they took the risk. If we want to have relationships with our children's children, if we want to find those relationships to be sources of joy and connection, their parents have to trust us and the world enough to let go a little, enough to relax and find pleasure in raising them and sharing them with the larger "village" to be raised.

I asked *The Mom Hour* community how they feel individuals from the older generation could help create a more supportive environment for today's parents, and was I heartened, inspired, and occasionally chastened by the simplicity and wisdom of their responses. Here is what I learned.

Empathy goes a long way.

Do you remember what it was like to have a small baby? I'll be honest—I don't. I *think* I do, but in reality, my memories are filtered heavily through time and my own nostalgia. So my attempts to relate to younger moms, no matter how well intentioned, are always going to be distorted by a sort of rose-colored amnesia that can be distinctly unhelpful to an overwhelmed mom.

"Shifting from 'You'll miss these days, I do!' to 'Ah, I remember those days! They were hard! You're doing great' would be huge for general society and individual interactions," wrote Darby, a member of The Mom Hour's Facebook community. "Older parents tend to just forget or see through rose-colored glasses," agreed Lindsey. "I don't really think parenting little ones is harder than it was when we were children, but the lack of empathy can be jarring."

We can show empathy not just through our words, but also in practical ways—like taking care not to schedule important family events when small kids are likely to be sleepy or wound up, or even in giving parents a pass to skip out of gatherings early if they're butting up against a bedtime.

Last, we can remind ourselves that today's generation of parents occupy a very different world from that of when our kids were little. Parenting culture is not what it was in the '90s or early 2000s. The bar on safety and health guidelines has been raised in many ways, parents are dealing with influences and pressures, and the economic reality is starkly different, as well. We can't fix all those ills for this generation, but reminding ourselves how different things are now can help us flex our empathy muscles.

Quit the "who had it worse" wars.

We may not have a seat at the table when important HR policies are being made, but being grumpy about family-friendly policies simply because we didn't benefit from them is the opposite of forward thinking or empathy.

Jesse has learned this the hard way. "Instead of feeling bitter about bad experiences you may have had when your kids were young because times were different, celebrate the changes with young moms and help normalize things like using pumping rooms, taking extended family leave, and talking about our families instead of trying to hide the real reason you're going to be gone next Tuesday," she suggested.

Mary adds this: "When my husband takes paternity leave, the older generation seems quick to remind me that it didn't exist when they were new moms and they did it all on their own." The result? She feels even guiltier for having much-needed help. "It would be so nice if the response could be 'How wonderful! I'm so glad that society is improving and acknowledging the necessary role of a father in the home. Those first few weeks are tough!'" she wrote.

"Advocate for policies that support parents who are still 'in the thick of it,' even when you would no longer benefit from such policies yourself," agreed Kassidy. "How many women argue against paid maternity leave, simply because they didn't receive it and don't think it's fair?"

I admit I sometimes look at younger parents, with all their gadgets and remote work possibilities, and wonder if they're getting a little soft. Certainly there is a conversation to be had about the way we've taught (or *not* taught) resilience to the younger generations who are now becoming, or considering becoming, parents. But there's a lot of nuance to the conversations about which generations had it "better" as parents. No matter which benefits or tools new parents might have that we didn't, the fact is that raising children is hard, and we should all take an interest in making it more doable. "It's not fair!" has no place in the conversation.

At least pretend to care about new parenting trends.

Overwhelmingly, younger moms are tired of having to explain, justify, or defend parenting choices, which I understand, because once upon a time I was very tired of having to explain, justify, and defend my own parenting choices! Social media has certainly amplified both the confusion around ideal parenting practices and the perceived judgment from others around everything from sleep training to the best time to start solids, and it can seem impossible to stay up to speed on every new practice.

But we can at least respect that our kids may do things very differently as parents from what we did, and we can also have some curiosity and interest about why. Most of the time emerging research or ideas about development have changed a practice over time; a younger parent's embrace of a new style of parenting isn't necessarily a judgment of how we did things. "Often if I am doing something different, it's built off of the things I learned from my own parents, just tweaked," wrote Shelby. "I would love for the older generation to approach younger parents by asking them questions about how they decided to do certain things."

Alexandra offered this approach: "One thing my mother-in-law has always done is say, 'What is the recommendation now?' for anything from starting solids to sleep or vaccines. I always really appreciated that it opened the door for me to be the 'expert' instead of her."

Alexandra's statement, and my initial gut reaction to it, revealed the real heart of the matter: *We still want to be the experts.* We put in the time; we worked so hard to learn so much, and it can feel like our knowledge is being mowed over or simply thrown away in the face of new trends. But I have to check myself there. The truth is, every generation does things differently from the one before; that doesn't mean it had no value. New generations build on the experience and information of the ones that came before them. We were experts in raising our own children, using the information that was available to us at the time. Yielding the role of "expert" on the latest studies and research isn't really a loss; it actually allows us to offer something even more important than data: wisdom.

We are still necessary (in other words, we're not done yet).

We put in our time... *now it's our time to really live.* That's the cultural message that's hard for exhausted parents coming out of the thick of intensive parenting not to embrace. And certainly there's some justification in taking a well-earned break after years of hands-on, arms-full childcare.

But for younger parents, the disconnection between generations can feel akin to abandonment.

"I am sure it is tempting to feel like, 'Whew, I did my time and now I'm going to enjoy my freedom now that my kids are older and I'm an empty nester,'" says Michelle. "But it means a lot when you find one of those people who are actually willing to sacrifice some of their hard-earned free time to help. At my church almost all the people who serve in the little kids' Sunday school class are parents of those same kids. It would be so nice if others who were out of that stage were more willing to help in these kinds of settings."

Kelsee shared this story: "When we moved into our neighborhood, a retired woman was telling me about a tradition that they had every year where the kids would decorate a specific tree in the neighborhood for Christmas. It sounded so fun when she was describing it to me, but then she finished by saying, 'I think it's time to hand this off to you moms so you can coordinate it.' My heart sunk. Needless to say, the tradition hasn't happened in the two years we've lived here—we young moms with small kids don't have the capacity or energy for arranging extra things like that. It was such a bummer to get this feeling of 'I can't be bothered to help with this anymore,' from someone who basically exclusively does leisure activities."

A young mother named Lauren summed it up by writing, "I think it would be helpful for the older generation to avoid falling into the trap of thinking along the lines of 'I already did my time so now I will only help when I feel like it' when it comes to young kids. We need the older generation to help those of us who are currently parenting—especially in a group setting like church or other community groups. I think it's important for the older generation to view themselves as still part of the 'raising littles' community. I think it's generally a mindset. Instead of viewing themselves as 'done' or 'out' once they have grown kids, why not view the situation as 'Now that my own hands are free, how can I use them to help others?'"

Reading the responses from this passionate and smart group of mothers, I felt a mix of recognition, inspiration—and, I'll admit, a few bursts of indignation. Why should I be expected to work the church nursery when I already did my time or keep holiday traditions going for younger parents if they don't value it enough to make the time for it themselves?

But once I breathed through the defensiveness for a moment, I realized what these young mothers are really saying. They aren't asking the older generation—which, I need to recognize, now includes me—to step in and do their parenting for them; they aren't specifically pointing a finger at any one elder for failing to show up. They're rightfully, I think, pointing to a societal dynamic in which generations have become isolated from each other, who see each other's challenges as irrelevant obstacles to their own goals, progress, and self-actualization.

Of course, it goes both ways. I hear daily from parents my own age who feel kept at arm's length from their adult kids, especially those who are starting families of their own. If we don't feel welcomed, if we don't feel relevant, if we don't feel like we have a place, what can we do about it but immerse ourselves in our careers and creative projects, our friends and pets and travel?

Here's the truth, though: remaining a part of our adult kids' lives, particularly their introduction to parenthood, won't necessarily be comfortable or easy. And here's another thing: it's not always their job to make it that way. We have to meet them halfway, possibly more than halfway, swallow our pride, pat down the chip on our own shoulders, and be open to expanding on what we think we know.

This is nothing new, after all. As new parents we had to learn to approach the small people in our lives with curiosity, compassion, and empathy. We had to learn new skills, be open to questioning our own upbringing, and overcome limiting family-of-origin stories. And most of all, we had to learn not to take it personally when our kids didn't make it easy on us. We'd do well, in this strange and stressful new world we must all coinhabit now, to take a page from our own parenting book and apply it to the way we relate to the younger generation as they also become parents. Our kids will eventually become adults, but when it comes to our relationships, we will always be the adults in the room. We need to act like it.

So what do we do? I don't think it has to be complicated. And we don't have to do all the things. What I hear from the young moms in my community is that a little bit of effort makes a big difference. And you don't have to be an actual grandparent (yet) to take on the role of helper, mentor, and support system to the younger generation of parents.

Take this example from Joan Marie, who is part of a support group for new moms started by women in the community with college-age kids. "They do the scheduling, they bring toys, snacks, and blankets, and they help us moms find any and all resources that we need," she wrote. The help and support of these not-that-much-older women, she says, has been a huge help to the young moms in the community: "They have connected me with doctors, specialists, and even held my baby while I have made appointments. I am so grateful for those women, passing their knowledge and kindness down to us."

Feeling inspired? Yeah, me too. But if organizing a group isn't your thing, that doesn't mean you can't still act as an important means of support. *The Mom Hour* group shared multiple examples of this kind of one-on-one support: a retired neighbor who swings over to watch a set of twins while their mother is running errands, or another mother who babysits preschool-age kids while her own kids are in school. Even simply thinking of parents of younger kids—by extending a clear invite to little ones when organizing a neighborhood party, or offering kid-friendly toys and snacks at gatherings—made an impact.

Make parenting fun again.

Is it just me, or does modern-day parenting seem to be presented as a big drag? Well, we only have our own generation to blame, friends. We upped the stakes, raised the expectations, and amped up the anxiety surrounding parenting, and we haven't done much to sell the younger generation on why anyone would want to choose this path. While we may not be able to solve every burden of modern-day life, we can, at the very least, model a sense of enjoying life, of valuing the world we live in enough to make it better for future generations.

As I said at the beginning of this chapter, I don't want young people to be compelled to have kids; I want them to *want* to have kids. In order to want to be parents, young people have to see child-rearing as a pursuit worth giving up sleep and freedom and money for. They have to believe our world is worth fighting for enough to bring new people into it.

It goes without saying that in order to extend this sort of help, hospitality, and hope to younger parents, we have to have actual relationships with them. And in this fractured world, perhaps that's the hardest part. It's awkward enough to offer help or extend an invitation to someone you know; it's downright impossible when you don't ever interact with people outside your age group to begin with. I am as guilty as anyone of holing up in the comfy little worlds I've created for myself, worlds that tend to be populated by people around my age and situation in life. But I also recognize that true community-building requires more diversity: of age, of family status, of worldview and background. Social media may provide us with helpful tools to spread the word about what we're doing in our real worlds, but make no mistake: these relationships have to start in the third dimension.

It's important to remember, I think, that marketers have a vested interest in keeping us all separate and consumptive: young people spending money on a hedonistic and career-driven lifestyle; parents spending money on conveniences, gadgets, and services to make child-rearing more manageable; and older people spending money to make up for lost leisure time, to relax, and to look and feel more youthful. If we started sharing resources with one another too much, particularly across generational lines, we wouldn't need to spend as much money on those conveniences, gadgets, and services.

Marketers benefit from selling us lifestyles that keep us living—and *spending*—separately.

One thing is clear to me: we need to push back against the siloing of generations and start reaching out if we ever want to start fixing what's wrong with modern family life. I need the reminder as much as anyone that there's room for generational community-building in my new, hands-free life. In fact, it may prove to be the best part of the rest of my life.

THE TIME WE'VE HAD, THE TIME WE HAVE

For a parent, there's perhaps nothing as confounding as the concept of time.

When children are small, the monotonous minutes—picking up the same toys again and again, reading the same books over and over—can seem to stretch into months. But look back at a year of your child's life, and those same months seem compressed into mere moments.

When my children were young, my relationship with time had an anxious, adversarial flavor. I hoarded it: five minutes here, ten there, cobbling together my life outside of caretaking in its margins. Five minutes could be used to surf the internet; fifteen was plenty of time for a shower. An hour to myself, with a soundly napping baby and no urgent needs from an older child? I could basically fit in a day's worth of work.

In the evenings my frenetic pace shifted to making dinner, managing homework and reading logs, and trying to stay ahead of the mess. Before I knew it, bedtime had come. I always wanted to be the mom who had both the time and the calm, steady energy for a leisurely bedtime reading and tuck-in session, but too many nights, I wasn't that mom. There was just too much to do and never enough hours in which to do it.

"*I don't have time, I don't have time, I don't have time*" became the drumbeat that propelled my life forward. In those days, all opportunities, offers, and obligations were filtered through a reality—or, at least, the perception of a reality—in which time was a scarce and precious resource that could only be spent on activities with a clear ROI. For a while I resented and resisted outside activities—a Tuesday-night swim meet or volunteer meeting felt like war on my efforts to keep all the balls in the air.

As I look back, it's hard not to breathe a sigh of regret over all the time I squandered trying to save time. We're all familiar with platitudes and poems extolling the virtues of slowing down to enjoy the quiet and messy moments rather than focusing on getting things done. They're annoying, but there's also an element of undeniable truth to them—which is probably why they're so annoying.

Because even though we all, in the throes of early motherhood, knew in our hearts that "it goes so fast" and "babies don't keep," we were also caught up in the forward thrust of Real Life happening all around us. Our own ambitions, whether they were career focused or personal, mattered to us; our families' needs for food, shelter, clothing, and a reasonably functional and clean home might have taken precedence over rocking that baby. There was no fairy mothering godmother to tell us exactly how to slow down, let things go, prioritize; we made decisions in the moment, and probably we could sometimes have made better ones.

The guilt and conflict and regret baked in around how we spend our time as parents seems unavoidable. No matter what, there will never be enough time, and we will never have spent the time we had exactly right.

You might think I've gotten better at this as my kids have gotten older...but have I really? I have more available time for myself than I've ever had before, and less remaining time with each of them than I ever had before—and yet I flip-flop back and forth between impatience and appreciation, between wanting to savor each moment and needing to *get on with it already*. After a holiday or vacation, no matter how much engagement and fun and joy we squeezed into every available minute, at the end I'm nearly always left with the uncomfortable feeling that, somewhere along the line, I squandered the time we had together.

After two and a half decades of complete immersion in motherhood—with days that sometimes moved so slowly I wanted to crawl out of my skin—time now seems to be moving along at a much quicker pace. For years, midlife and all that comes with it—from the freedom that accompanies kids getting older to the challenges of physical changes—felt more like a vague concept than something that would eventually actually happen. But it's all starting to feel very real, as more and more milestones appear on the horizon and then, in a blink, disappear in the rear-view mirror. And as the changes around me and in me compound and pick up speed, I find myself asking the question, "What's next?" with a lot more urgency.

I never used to think much about what happened in the years

after, say, forty-five or fifty. It seemed to me that all the action was in the first half of life: after all, that's when the self-discovering and mate selecting and baby making happens. And when I was looking forward to that, or in the thick of it, that's what I thought most about. I never really considered that there might be just as much action—just as much life to live—on the other side.

Now, of course, I'm starting to see things a bit differently, which I suppose is what happens at midlife. Yes, I have done a *lot* in my forty-seven years, many of those years with small kids in tow. But in a lot of ways, I'm just getting started. Assuming I reach my life expectancy—which I know is not guaranteed—I've got about thirty-five years left. If I live as long as both my maternal and paternal grandmothers, I'll be here twelve or thirteen years more than that. Enough, it turns out, to pack in quite a lot of living.

A decade ago, still in the arms-full stage of motherhood, I would have jealously guarded the luxurious amount of free time I have now. But maybe what I was really craving deep-down wasn't more productivity, but more space to breathe…and that's something I've found myself finally able to claim in midlife.

Yet I also know that, just as in my early mom days, time doesn't tame itself.

At one point in my life, I honed the fine art of squeezing every drop of productivity out of an hour because I had no other choice. These days I have more options and more white space, but I'm still operating within the reality that time is limited. I have dreams now just the same as then, and I owe it to myself to fit the most important ones into the available hours.

I expect that in my nineties, I'll still be wishing I had more time to do the things I want to do, while looking back and wondering how I used up all the time I had. But hopefully I'll always be grateful for the time left to come, regardless of whether I spend it doing or just being.

Whether I choose to cram those years full of new experiences or intentionally slow down the pace, my midlife years (and beyond) are full of possibilities, not just a slow sunset on the decades already lived. I've always known that logically, but sometimes it takes "doing the math" to help that truth set in.

As I consider "what's next" for me, I find myself looking both backward and forward. I'm grappling with the fact that there are certain possibilities that are now behind me for good while I'm also navigating the (many!) other possibilities that are still unfolding, offering so much promise. It's a heady, exciting space to inhabit. It's also more than a little overwhelming.

Wrapping up this book, I find myself reflecting on the time I've spent so far in my life as a mother. On the one hand, I hold the knowledge I wish I'd had when my kids were little: that time slips past more quickly than you can imagine; that the things we believe to be so urgent in the moment are often not nearly as important as they seem. On the other hand, I hold the reality that, even now, I'm simply doing what I've always done: trying to stay on top of everything I must do while making space for the things that matter most. I won't always get the balance right, but it's still worth making the effort.

A month after I finished the initial draft of this book, Eric, Owen, and I journeyed north to Houghton, MI, for Michigan Tech's freshman welcome weekend. The itinerary included moving Owen into his dorm, sharing a meal in the campus dining hall, and attending a welcome reception for incoming freshmen. But the weekend took an unexpected, and unwelcome, turn. After bringing Owen's stuff up to his dorm room, Eric and I decided to walk into town for a while to give him and his new roommate a chance to get to know each other—and on that walk, I somehow managed to roll, and badly sprain, my ankle. Instead of participating in move-in festivities that evening, I wound up in the emergency room getting an x-ray. And instead of the ceremonious, poignant goodbye I'd envisioned the next morning—complete with an Instagram-worthy photo—Owen and I shared an awkward hug through the car door, where my ankle was propped up on pillows in the backseat for the long ride home.

Ceremonious it was not, but the anticlimactic send-off was certainly emotional…at least, for me. I cried harder than I'd like to admit as Owen walked slowly across the parking lot to join the rest of the freshmen gathering in a grassy area for a welcome-weekend assembly. It felt so unfair: rather than getting to participate in the excitement of the moment I'd helped bring him to, I was literally sidelined. I felt thwarted, left-out, almost—irrationally, I know—*rejected*. And while this wasn't my first (or even my third!) time letting a child go, something about the experience this time around, with all the other huge changes happening in our lives, felt particularly fraught.

But in the ensuing weeks, both my ankle and heart slowly healed as our downsized family settled into a new, quieter routine—one that opened up surprising new opportunities for connection: with no older brother to absorb her time and attention, Clara has more of both for me; and we spend a lot more time together, watching TV and just hanging out. Eric and I have more time for each other, and I have more time to myself, too, time I didn't perhaps realize I needed. (It's easy to underestimate the amount of emotional energy it can require to help a young adult launch to their next phase of life until they're gone and you have a moment to look around you, breathe, and think, *Wow, that was a lot.*)

As I have with the other three grown-and-flown boys, I find myself navigating a delicate mothering-from-a-distance dance with Owen. I try to be available yet undemanding, nurturing but not needy. I'm sure I step all over his toes all the time anyway, but he—and my other kids—seem to be figuring out these stages of their lives regardless…and so am I.

Rereading this manuscript now, just a few months after finishing it, it strikes me how different I, and my family, have already become in a short amount of time. And by the time this book is in your hands—or has been passed on to a friend, or has sat on the library shelf for a while (hopefully not *too* long)—my life as a mother, and yours, will have changed again, and again, and again. To truly embrace the role of a parent is to accept that nothing stays the same. Perhaps the best thing we can do is to hold on with a loving but loose grip, so we can all feel free to become the next version of ourselves.

The hands-free stage of motherhood presents us with an opportunity to do something radical: to turn all that nurturing energy we've spent years or decades giving others and turn it back around toward ourselves. It's an opportunity to examine the way we've parented so far, to experience and honor our regrets and make amends if needed. It's an opportunity to rewire mental pathways that have become stuck in old ways of doing things. It's an opportunity to renegotiate our dynamics with our kids and friends and spouses. It's an opportunity to invest in our creativity, reimagine our future identity, and mourn and release past identities. It's also an opportunity to explore new ways of relating to generations coming up behind us, growing into roles even more valuable and expansive than the ones we filled as the heads of our own households. It may just be an opportunity, in fact, to change the world.

Motherhood, as both an identity and a way of relating to others, has been the single greatest gift of my life, and it's the essence of myself that I intend to carry along with me into this next stage. I can't wait to see where it takes me—and you—next.

ACKNOWLEDGMENTS

While I was writing this book, it struck me over and over again how much I've grown as a human being in the process of raising five other human beings. To my wonderful, funny, and completely adorable crew—Jacob, Isaac, William, Owen, and Clara—thank you for teaching me how to be a mother, for continuing to let me crash the party when you're all hanging out together, and for responding to my texts…most of the time.

Thank you to my older sister, Kathreen, who paved the way and showed me how to nurse babies with no hands, chase toddlers through Target, and raise teenagers without losing your sense of humor. You were my first role model as a mom.

To Sarah, my ten-year podcast cohost and business bestie, who did me the huge favor of hashing out so many of these topics with me on-air, in real time—thank you. Your intentionality, thoughtfulness, and presence have had a profound impact on my life and motherhood.

Thank you to Jenna and Melissa (Missy) for being there, over and over. It has been an honor to come of age together with the two of you, first as teenagers, then as mothers, and now as midlife women. Here's to early bedtimes, magnesium supplements, and whatever else is next.

To the mothers I've known throughout my life, those still living and those now passed, whose wisdom and perspective my family has benefited from throughout the years, thank you. And a big thanks as well to the women of The Kettle community and The Mom Hour community for sharing your experiences and insights over the years.

Thank you to Kerry Sparks of Levine Greenberg Rostan Literary Agency, for understanding the beating heart of this book and for believing in me as its author; to Anna Michels for your thoughtful and sensitive editing; and for the whole team at Sourcebooks for bringing this book to life. It's been a pleasure working with all of you.

And last but certainly not least, thank you to Eric for keeping my mug always topped up with tea as I write. You are a true partner, and I'm grateful you're my person.

ABOUT THE AUTHOR

As a mother of five kids ages teen to young adult, a parenting writer for twenty-five years, and the cohost of *The Mom Hour* podcast, which has been in constant publication for ten years and downloaded over fifteen million times, Meagan Francis has long been a strong advocate for women and mothers and a celebrated voice in the parenting community, with the clear messages: motherhood doesn't have to be miserable, and it's all gonna be okay. Meagan lives in Michigan. Her writing and podcasts can be found at meaganfrancis.com.